W9-BKL-176

"*Pursuing God's Will Together* is a much-needed corrective to our headstrong individualism today. It drills down deep into rock-bed practicalities for any community seeking to discern the will of God together. I recommend it highly."

RICHARD J. FOSTER, author, *Celebration of Discipline* and *Sanctuary of the Soul*

"This book needs a warning label: 'Content may be disruptive to your understanding of Christian life, leadership and community.' Ruth Haley Barton has provided every Christian with an invaluable resource for discerning and fulfilling the purposes of God. In a world where Christians and Christian leadership and communities have largely succumbed to secular processes for decision making, Barton brings a clear, challenging and compelling call for a radical alternative. This book is not the product of a 'theorist,' but the mature distillation of Barton's own journey into a life hid with Christ in God for the sake of others. This is a must-read for every Christian leader and leadership group, and a primer for every Christian."

M. ROBERT MULHOLLAND JR., professor emeritus, Asbury Theological Seminary, and author, *Invitation to a Journey* and *The Deeper Journey*

"Ruth Haley Barton knows only too well that discerning God's will requires a personal commitment to transformation as well as an openness to engage in a group process. In *Pursuing God's Will Together,* she shows us in a systematic way how it's done. Every Christian leader will benefit from such a practical approach to such an ancient practice."

ALBERT HAASE, O.F.M., author, *This Sacred Moment*

"It's impossible to overstate how needed, valuable, timely and timeless this book is. It is as wise as Methuselah and as practical as a slingshot. Ruth has rendered a massive service to church leaders everywhere, and to all the churches they lead. Herein lies the remedy for the sad but common malady we see today: otherwise godly men and women pursuing God's kingdom with worldly navigational equipment. I plan to buy a case of *Pursuing God's Will Together* upon its release and make it mandatory reading for all of our leaders. It can hardly come soon enough."

MARK BUCHANAN, pastor, New Life Community Baptist Church, and author, *Spiritual Rhythm* and *Your Church Is Too Safe*

"In *Pursuing God's Will Together* [Ruth Haley Barton] weaves her own wisdom with others in bringing forth a beautiful tapestry of spirituality in community."

CHUCK OLSEN, founder, Worshipful-Work, and author, *Transforming Church Boards*

"Ruth Haley Barton has identified an important issue in spiritual leadership and in how we make decisions, revealing where our integrity as leaders lies. Do we really believe that God has something to say, by his Holy Spirit, in terms of what direction we take? Ruth does a great job of describing practices that can help teams become more adept at hearing God's voice in the practical areas of leading and serving."

DOUG NUENKE, U.S. director, The Navigators

"I like this book. It is wise, thoughtful, gracious and a little bit disturbing—Ruth will surely upset some of your preconceived notions. If you are like me, you believe in the guidance of the Holy Spirit, but you want to be wise and not presumptuous about knowing God's will for your group. This book is a real gift to folks like us. It provides us with much more than simply a plan of action. You can use it yourself, but it will also be quite useful to you with your fellow decision makers, so that discerning God's will together becomes an experience in spiritual growth for the whole team."

JOHN YATES, rector, The Falls Church

"Ruth Haley Barton is a gifted distiller of historic best practices for community discernment and direction. Exercising her counsel on the rare 'vow of stability' would by itself rescue multiple organizations from broken strategic trajectories. I highly recommend *Pursuing God's Will Together* for leaders, teams and organizations."

DR. BRUCE MCNICOL, president, Truefaced, Inc.

"*Pursuing God's Will Together* is a powerfully convicting and timely book for those of us who are fully aware that we are incapable of effective leadership apart from God's wisdom and direction. How to discern God's purposes individually and as a dynamic team is the genius of this compellingly creative call to kingdom movement. Ruth Haley Barton presents us with a proven—if at times painful—practice that can ultimately take our finite efforts to where our infinite God wants them to go."

HAROLD B. SMITH, president and CEO, Christianity Today International

"I have been grateful for Ruth Haley Barton's wisdom in the past on spiritual disciplines so crucial for the soul of a leader. I am sure her latest work will be of great benefit to those who seek the grace of discernment in their work and ministries."

GARY HAUGEN, president and CEO, International Justice Mission

"While there has been a revival of interest in spiritual disciplines for some time, there is precious little available about how to practice them in community. More specifically, there is almost nothing about helping Christian leaders discern God's presence and activities together. That is, until now. With *Pursuing God's Will Together,* Ruth Haley Barton—a recognized leader in spiritual formation—fills this need admirably. This is an important, unique book that will be sure to transform Christian corporate leadership from a pure business model to a more spiritually integrated approach. I highly recommend it."

J. P. MORELAND, professor of philosophy, Talbot School of Theology, Biola University, and author, *The God Question*

"Fabulous! I look forward to giving copies to our staff and elders. Ruth provides a practical, powerful road map so we can discern the most important question as a leadership team: What is God's will for us on a particular issue?"

PETE SCAZZERO, pastor, New Life Fellowship Church, and author, *The Emotionally Healthy Church*

PURSUING

GOD'S WILL

TOGETHER

A DISCERNMENT PRACTICE
FOR LEADERSHIP GROUPS

RUTH HALEY BARTON

IVP Books

An imprint of InterVarsity Press
Downers Grove, Illinois

InterVarsity Press
P.O. Box 1400, Downers Grove, IL 60515-1426
World Wide Web: www.ivpress.com
E-mail: email@ivpress.com

InterVarsity Press® is the book-publishing division of InterVarsity Christian Fellowship/USA®, a movement of students and faculty active on campus at hundreds of universities, colleges and schools of nursing in the United States of America, and a member movement of the International Fellowship of Evangelical Students. For information about local and regional activities, write Public Relations Dept., InterVarsity Christian Fellowship/USA, 6400 Schroeder Rd., P.O. Box 7895, Madison, WI 53707-7895, or visit the IVCF website at <www.intervarsity.org>.

Scripture quotations, unless otherwise noted, are from the New Revised Standard Version of the Bible, *copyright 1989 by the Division of Christian Education of the National Council of the Churches of Christ in the USA. Used by permission. All rights reserved.*

The closing prayer for chapter one is from J. Philip Newell, Celtic Treasure: Daily Scriptures and Prayers © 2005 Wm. B. Eerdmans Publishing Company, Grand Rapids, MI. Reprinted by permission of the publisher; all rights reserved.

The closing prayers for chapters two and three are from Guerrillas of Grace by Ted Loder copyright © 1984, 2004 Ted Loder, admin Augsburg Fortress. Reproduced by permission. All rights reserved.

The closing prayers for chapters four and seven, as well as the third and fourth lines of "A Prayer of Commitment" at the end of chapter eight, are adapted from © 2001 The Iona Community. Taken from The Iona Abbey Worship Book, Wild Goose Publications, Glasgow. Used by permission.

While all stories in this book are true, some names and identifying information in this book have been changed to protect the privacy of the individuals involved.

Cover design: Cindy Kiple
Images: © Steve Deer/Trevillion Images
Interior design: Beth Hagenberg

ISBN 978-0-8308-3566-9

Printed in the United States of America ∞

Library of Congress Cataloging-in-Publication Data

Barton, R. Ruth, 1960
 Pursuing God's will together : a discernment practice for leadership groups / Ruth Haley Barton.
     p. cm.
 Includes bibliographical references (p.   ).
 ISBN 978-0-8308-3566-9 (hardcover : alk. paper)
 1. Christian leadership. 2. Church group work. 3. Discernment (Christian theology) 4. Decision making—Religious aspects—Christianity. I. Title.
 BV652.1.B373 2012
 253'.7—dc23

2012005246

P	17	16	15	14	13	12	11	10	9	8	7	6	5	4	3	2	1
Y	26	25	24	23	22	21	20	19	18	17	16	15	14	13	12		

To my grandsons

Gabriel Anthony, Thomas Ryan and Finley Brant

May you grow up to be young men who are ever-committed to discerning and doing the will of God.

And to the leadership community of the Transforming Center

You have given me a place to fully live into the realities and practices described in this book.

I am forever grateful. This one's for you.

*The question is deceptively simple to ask
and exquisitely difficult to answer:
Am I truly seeking to do Thy will . . . or mine?*

GERALD MAY

❧

CONTENTS

Introduction

The Heart of Spiritual Leadership

Decision making has its limits. We make decisions.
Discernment is given. The Spirit of God, which operates
at the deepest levels of the human psyche and within
the mysteries of the faith community,
brings to the surface gifts of wisdom and guidance
which we can only discover and name.

Danny Morris and Chuck Olsen

It was a conversation similar to many I have had with Christian leaders. An associate pastor from a large church was telling me that his church was going through a major transition as its leaders tried to respond to its growth. They had outgrown their facility (a good problem to have!), so the obvious question was, Will we add on to our facility or will we start another church?

As we talked, it became clear that this question was only the tip of the iceberg. Beneath the surface larger questions lurked: What should be our emphasis now? Does our mission still capture what we feel called to? Is our leadership structure effective for what is emerging now? Can we keep going at this pace, or will we burn ourselves out by adding a building campaign and more people and activities to our plates?

Sensing the weight this pastor was carrying, I probed a little deeper and asked, "How are you going about answering these questions together? Do you have a clearly articulated process for discerning God's will in these matters?" A look of disorientation crossed his face as he realized that the answer to the question was no. After recovering a bit, he added, "But we always have a time of prayer at the beginning of our meetings!"

It was awkward, to say the least.

This pastor, like so many Christian leaders, had a vague sense that our approach to decision making should be different from secular models—particularly when we are leading a church or an organization with a spiritual purpose.[1] The problem is that we're not quite sure what that difference is. In the absence of a clear consensus, that difference often gets reduced to an obligatory devotional (often viewed as irrelevant to the business portion of the meeting) *or* the perfunctory prayers that bookend the meeting. Sometimes even these well-meaning attempts at a spiritual focus get lost in the shuffle!

LEADERSHIP DISCERNMENT

Discernment, in a most general sense, is the capacity to recognize and respond to the presence and the activity of God—both in the ordinary moments and in the larger decisions of our lives. The apostle Paul says that we are to be transformed by the renewing of our minds *so that* we can discern what the will of God is, that which is good, acceptable and perfect (Rom 12:2). This includes not only the mind of each individual but also the corporate mind.

Discernment literally means *to separate, to discriminate, to determine, to decide* or *to distinguish* between two things. Spiritual discernment is the ability to distinguish or discriminate between good (that which is of God and draws us closer to God) and evil (that which is not of God and draws us away from God). There are many qualities that contribute to good leadership, but it is our commitment to *discerning and doing the will of God* through the help of the Holy Spirit that distinguishes spiritual leadership from other kinds of leadership.

Corporate or leadership discernment, then, is the capacity to recognize and respond to the presence and activity of God *as a leadership group* relative to the issues we are facing, and to make decisions in response to that Presence. Spiritual leaders are distinguished by their commitment to discern important matters together so they can affirm a shared sense of God's desire for them and move forward on that basis.

It is hard to imagine that spiritual leadership could be about anything *but* seeking to know and do the will of God, and yet many leadership groups do not have this as their clear mandate and reason for existence. This raises a serious question: If we are not pursuing the will of God together in fairly intentional ways, what are we *doing?* Our own will? What seems best according to our own thinking and planning? That which is merely strategic or expedient or good for the ego?

Discernment together as leaders, on the other hand, opens us to an entirely different reality—the wisdom of God that is beyond human wisdom and is available to us as we learn how to open ourselves to it (1 Cor 2:6-16). This approach to leadership presents unique challenges because it requires us to move beyond reliance on human thinking and strategizing to a place of deep listening and response to the Spirit of God within and among us. This is not to dismiss what human wisdom and strategic thinking have to offer us. Our ability to think things through and apply reason to our decision making is a gift from God; however, the Scriptures are clear that human wisdom and the wisdom of God are not the same thing. Part of becoming more discerning is the ability to distinguish between the two (1 Cor 1:18-31).

One of the challenges to leadership discernment is that it can seem somewhat subjective and even mystical, which doesn't always go over too well with hard-nosed business people and pragmatists—those who often make up boards and other leadership groups. It is one thing to rely on what feels like a more subjective approach when it pertains to our personal life, but it feels much riskier when our decisions involve large budgets, other people's financial investments, the lives of multiple staff, reports to high-powered boards and serving a "customer base" (congregation or organization) with varying levels of expectation. And yet many leaders today are longing for a way of leading that is more deeply responsive to the will of God than to the latest ideas from a *New York Times* bestseller. We wonder, *Is there a trustworthy process that enables Christian leaders to actively seek God relative to decisions we are making?*

The answer is a resounding yes! and it is why I have written this book—to provide practical guidance for leaders and leadership teams who want to enter more deeply into the process of corporate discernment as a way of life in leadership.

Personal Reflection

How do you respond to the idea that discernment is what distinguishes spiritual leadership from other kinds of leadership? How would you describe the way your leadership group makes decisions currently?

A ONE-STOP SHOP FOR LEADERSHIP GROUPS

While there are many books on personal discernment and a few resources on corporate discernment, this book is designed to be a one-stop-shop guide for leadership groups who wish to become a community for discernment. The process involves (1) preparing individual leaders for discernment, (2) becoming a community for discernment at the leadership level and (3) engaging an actual process for discerning God's will together as leaders. This integration of spiritual transformation, community and discernment is based in part on Romans 12:2, in which Paul establishes a strong cause-and-effect relationship between spiritual transformation and the ability to discern and do the will of God in the context of the new community of believers gathered in Rome: "Do not be conformed to this world, but be transformed by the renewing of your minds, *so that* you may discern what is the will of God, what is good and acceptable and perfect" (emphasis added).

For the purposes of this book I have not made a strong distinction between churches and Christian ministry organizations because I believe that whenever and wherever Christians gather in Christ's name to carry out his purposes in the world, we are the body of Christ. As an expression of Christ's presence on earth there should be something about what we do and how we do it that is distinctly spiritual. Thus, when I use the word *church* or *community*, I am referring to any group of Christians who gather in the name of Christ and are seeking to be responsive to Christ's purposes in the world. Whenever Christians gather we are, at the deepest level of reality, the community of Jesus (Mk 3:34-35), and we have the opportunity to make decisions in a way that reflects this reality. This book is intended, then, for leadership groups in churches and Christian organizations who are ready to be more intentional about becoming a spiritual community that exists to discern and do the will of God.

PREPARATION AND PROCESS
One of the things I have learned in my own practice of corporate discernment, and also in working with others, is that *the preparation*

is actually more important than the process. If leaders and communities of leaders are prepared at the levels put forth in this book, discernment will happen even without a process. Conversely, if leaders are not prepared on the levels described here, there is a good chance discernment won't happen even when they engage the process; there are too many human dynamics that will get in the way. *That's why two-thirds of the book is about preparation and one-third is about the actual practice of leadership discernment.* It is also why the book is designed to function on two levels at once—to create space for each person's *personal* journey of transformation and growth in discernment, while at the same time providing guidance for the *group process* of leadership discernment. Thus, you will find questions for personal reflection throughout each chapter, indicated by a gray box; then, when you convene as a group, there is an exercise for processing and practicing together at the end of each chapter.

Becoming a community for discernment at the leadership level will not happen by accident because there are so many internal and external forces at work pulling us in other directions. What exactly is involved in shaping a group of leaders into a group who can together discern God's will?

First, a leadership group needs to have a *shared understanding* of what discernment is, a *shared conviction* that discernment is the heart of spiritual leadership, and a *shared affirmation* that discerning and doing the will of God is how they intend to lead. This in itself is no small thing.

Often, when individuals are invited to serve as elders, deacons or board members in churches and organizations, the definition of spiritual leadership is assumed or (at best) it is very general, and the expectations for what that means are unclear and ill-defined. That is why it is important to take time to establish a biblical understanding and vision for discernment as the heart of spiritual leadership. This includes understanding what the inner obstacles to such an approach might be, which is the focus of chapter one. If you take time with this chapter, you can establish commitment to discernment as a group norm that will serve you well in the long run—far beyond your current leadership group. Even if your leadership group has rotating terms, the group identity, norms and expectations will have been clearly established so that those who rotate on know what they are joining and are shaped by that reality.

The rest of the book is structured in two parts: becoming a community for discernment, and exploring an actual practice for leadership discernment. Chapters one through three focus on *the spiritual preparation of each individual leader.* Chapters four through eight address *the preparation of the leadership group as a community for discernment.* And chapters nine to twelve *describe the process of leadership discernment,* giving you a chance to begin exploring it together.

To flesh out what the process of becoming a community for discernment looks like in the life of a group, I have included (starting in chapter two) the story of a group of leaders from Grace Church as a thread running throughout the book. The group itself is fictitious, and yet it is all true; everything that happens in the group is based on experiences I have had facilitating leaders from various churches and organizations in preparing for and practicing leadership discernment. This group discovers what we all have a chance to discover: that corporate discernment, like all spiritual disciplines, is a concrete practice that opens us to the surprising activity of God in our lives. And *that*, friends, is when leadership gets exciting!

A WORD OF PASTORAL CONCERN

I know that leaders today are tired. Tired from within because their ministry leadership is often carried out in the context of schedules that are too full and barely sustainable. Tired from without because of the continual burden of responsibility and expectation others place on them, and which they accept. Tired from beyond because current models for ministry get them ramped up to do and be more than they can realistically do and be, and yet they are still trying.

This book is not meant to add to the exhaustion. Instead, it is meant to provide hope that there is a way of doing life in leadership that is not so complicated and heavy—a way of making decisions that does not have to rely on our own brilliance and ability to think hard, a way of being involved in God's work that ends up being more about God's work than our own. Discerning and doing the will of God together is that way.

So I invite you to relax. Read the book with your spiritual heart first, and start discerning now. Don't let your first question be, *Will this work in my setting?* as though the particularities of your setting—your organizational structure, your church polity, your problems, your people—are the norm against which all reality is to be measured. Instead, ask, *Is it good? Is there a sense of rightness to it? Does it draw me (and us) toward the good—toward God?* If your group can agree on that much, the rest will come.

Yes, there will be some new steps to learn, some new things to practice. Feel free to do *something* before you do *everything;* pick the one thing you think you can do, and do it with all your heart. God faithfully comes into any bit of space we create for him, and pretty soon the one thing you do before you do everything leads to another thing and another, until you find that leadership is not the burden it once was. It is a dance in which God leads and you follow. It is a wave that God sends, and you ride it. It is the breath of God, and you are the feather that floats upon it. It is a wind of the Spirit that blows, and you lift your sail to catch it. It is a powerful current that is already flowing, and *you* are in that flow.

PART ONE

BECOMING A

COMMUNITY FOR

DISCERNMENT

1

LEARNING TO SEE

Most people do not see things as they are;
rather, they see things as they are.

RICHARD ROHR

Several years ago I had Lasik surgery—a pretty big deal for someone who has worn glasses or contacts since fifth grade. I had heard about Lasik surgery for years and had thought of having it done, but it was expensive and I couldn't really believe that it was as good as it sounded. Well, at some point I got tired of how complicated seeing had become for me, and I decided to do it. And guess what? It was as good as it sounded! I walked into the surgery center not being able to see without glasses or contacts, and I walked out being able to see everything with my own eyes. No glasses, no contacts, nothing. Whether it came at the hands of a skilled doctor or Jesus himself touching my eyes, it felt like a miracle to me. What an amazing feeling it was to be able to see in a way I had never seen before! "Once I was blind, but now I see" took on a whole new meaning.

THE TROUBLE WITH SEEING

One of the miracles Jesus most commonly performed while he was on this earth was the healing of blind people. The reason this particular miracle was so common might have to do with the fact that it is a metaphor for the spiritual journey itself—the movement from spiritual blindness to spiritual sight. In fact, the spiritual journey can be understood as the movement from seeing God nowhere, or seeing God only where we expect to see him, to seeing God everywhere, especially where we least expect him.

Ignatius of Loyola, founder of the Jesuits and best known for developing a set of spiritual exercises intended to hone people's capacity to see and respond to God in all of life, defined the aim of discernment as "finding God in *all* things in order that we might love and serve God in all" (emphasis added). Discernment is an ever-increasing capacity to "see" or discern the works of God in the midst of the human situation so that we can align ourselves with whatever it is that God is doing. Every Christian is called to this kind of discernment (Rom 12:2). It is a mark of Christian maturity (1 Jn 4:1), and it is also a spiritual gift with which some individuals in the body of Christ are particularly graced (1 Cor 12:10).

Discernment together as leaders takes us beyond the personal to an increasing capacity to "see" what God is up to in the place we are called to lead. It calls us to be courageous in seeking the will of God and then making decisions that are responsive to that will as it unfolds in front of us. There is a great deal of biblical precedent for discernment together as leaders. Acts 6:1-7 records a situation in which the apostles needed to discern God's heart and mind regarding the complaints of a minority. Acts 15:19-20 describes a major decision involving doctrine and practice that needed to be discerned. Acts 21:10-14 records a situation in which an individual in the group (Paul) was contemplating a personal decision that would affect the leadership group he was a part of, and so he opened up that decision to a shared discernment process.

All these passages recount situations in which believers in the New Testament church, through the presence of the Holy Spirit, discerned God's will regarding important decisions; this, however, is not always as easy as it sounds.

John 9 records the account of a group of very religious people who were unable to recognize the work of God in their midst and thus *missed* the opportunity to be a part of what God was doing. In fact, the religious *leaders* were most guilty of thwarting and eventually dismissing the work of God taking place among them. In this particular story the bulk of the attention is given to the varying levels of spiritual blindness among those who witnessed the healing of a blind man. Everyone in this story saw the same man healed (or saw evidence of it), but all of them had difficulty recognizing and naming it as the work of God. What should have been a day of uproarious celebration for the healed man deteriorated into a day of controversy, debate, fear and expulsion. What prevented his family, friends and neighbors from recognizing and responding to the presence and activity of God in their midst is not all that different from what prevents us from seeing God's work today.

ASKING THE WRONG QUESTION
The story begins with really good news: Jesus *saw* the blind man, and being seen by Jesus opens up tremendous potential for healing. However, the story goes rapidly downhill from there because those who should have been seeing spiritual reality most clearly were the most blind and undiscerning. Sadly, those who were most "spiritual" were the ones who were most out of touch with God's heart for this situation.

The disciples who were with Jesus saw the blind man too, but they used this man's misfortune as an opportunity for theological and philosophical discussion. "Who sinned, this man or his parents?" There was no love, no compassion for this man's situation, no concern for his well-being. Instead they turned him into an object lesson, reducing him to a specimen in order to satiate their own intellectual curiosity. They distanced themselves from the raw humanity of the situation *and* from their own calling as Christ followers to make a compassionate response. Instead of seeing this as an occasion to care for another human being and to wonder about the spiritual possibilities present in the situation, they added insult to injury by asking the blame question: *Whose fault is it that this happened?*

The disciples, for all of their closeness to Jesus, were caught in a kind of blindness that was more limiting and debilitating than physical blindness. It was a *structural blindness* embedded in the belief system they adhered to. The question they asked was shaped by their outdated religious beliefs and cultural superstitions—the commonly held assumption that human misfortune had to be someone's fault. And it framed the situation so narrowly that it only allowed for two outcomes, neither of which was positive. Either the blind man sinned or his parents sinned. The only way they could have seen beyond these assumptions and their implications would have been to somehow stand outside the system and the limits of their shared way of thinking.

Jesus responded by saying (in effect), "You are asking the wrong question. Neither this man nor his parents sinned. That is an old way of seeing and interpreting reality, and has nothing to do with spiritual reality as it is unfolding right now. *This man was born blind so the works of God could be revealed in and through his life.*" This possibility hadn't occurred to them because their systemic way of thinking had produced the wrong question in the first place. The right question, according to Jesus, was, What is God doing in this situation, and how can I get on board with it? Now *that* is a much better question. In fact, it is the best possible question in the face of the brokenness and impossibility of the human situation.

Jesus was not trying to sugarcoat the situation or to avoid dealing with the harsh realities of life. Yes, there is evil in the world. Yes, there is sin with all of its tragic consequences. Yes, there is a complex web of cause-and-effect relationships at work in the human experience. But what good does the blame question do? The real question is, What is God going to do with it? Jesus engaged the heartbreak and the complexity of the human situation by pointing out that such situations create the most amazing possibilities for God to be at work. He said, "Let's learn how to notice *that* and then get involved." Which is exactly what he did.

One of the first lessons we learn about discernment—from Jesus, anyway—is that it will always tend toward concrete expressions of love with real people rather than theoretical conversations about theology and philosophy. Such conversations are valuable *only* if they eventually lead us to more concrete expressions of love for the real people who are in need around us. If such conversations don't move us toward concrete action in the world, we become the proverbial noisy gong and clashing symbol. The disciples' blindness to the work of God in their midst is sobering because it demonstrates that even those who are closest to Jesus and on a serious spiritual journey can still miss things—especially if we are living and breathing the same cultural influences together.

STUCK IN OLD PARADIGMS

The blind man's neighbors were the next group of people given the opportunity to recognize the work of God in their midst. They had seen the blind man every day and were intimate with the situation. Perhaps some of them were even friends of the family who had been there the day he was born and shared his parents' grief when they discovered he was blind. They had pretty strong ideas about what the situation was and were stuck in their paradigms. A blind man who could now see—particularly this blind man, whom they knew so well—just did not fit what they were accustomed to seeing, so they couldn't "see" it.

The neighbors were afflicted, as we all are, with cognitive filters that helped them categorize and make sense of reality. The problem of course is that these unconscious filters, developed over years of interacting with the situation in the same way, prevented them from seeing anything new or allowing any new data into their consciousness. They found ways to talk themselves out of this new possibility by questioning whether the healed man was their neighbor, even though the man himself was right there saying, "Hey, it's me!" If the situation wasn't so sad, it would be comical.

The neighbors' predicament points out another difficulty we have with seeing: we only see what we are ready to see, expect to see and even desire to see. And we're even more stuck when we are with others who share the same paradigms. How desperately we need practices, experiences and questions that help us get outside our paradigms so that we can see old realities in new ways!

PRESERVING THE SYSTEM AT ALL COSTS

By now the situation had gotten so confusing the neighbors didn't even trust themselves; they brought the man to the Pharisees to seek help in making sense of it all. The Pharisees were the most committed followers of God in their day. Their job, which they took very seriously, was to uphold and restore a deeper piety and holiness to the Jewish people in the only way they knew how— through a meticulous observance of the law. The Pharisees were by-the-book people. They were determined to be right. But, as I once heard Dallas Willard say, "It is hard to be right and not hurt anyone with it!"

On the day of the blind man's healing the Pharisees had only one concern: the preservation of the religious system (as represented by the issue of sabbath keeping) and their place of power within it. As long as the system remained clearly defined and everyone was functioning according to its rules and expectations, they remained safe and in control.

The religious system also afforded them an easy, straight-forward way of evaluating themselves and others—by the externals of laws and rituals, religious beliefs and loyalty to the powers that be. Their strict adherence to this way of evaluating people made them judgmental and uncaring in the way they wielded the power of their position. The Pharisees did not hesitate to use their power to intimidate, exploit and exclude those who didn't toe the line wherever they chose to draw it. So on this most amazing day not one of them jumped up and gave the blind man a high five. Not one of them said, "How exciting for you!" No one was the least bit curious about what it was like to be able to see for the first time ever. No one asked to hear the details. Instead, they fought, and they fought hard, to preserve the system and to dismiss anything that threatened the system the way they understood it.

Getting caught up in preserving the system gave them a convenient way to avoid dealing with who Jesus was, the miracle he had performed and the fresh wind of the Spirit of God that was blowing among them. The Pharisees used the issue of sabbath keeping as a smoke screen to prevent them from facing the ways that Jesus' presence was messing with their system. Jesus clearly brought a different kind of authority than they had, and he was responding to a different set of priorities. In a desperate attempt to regain control of the situation, they attacked Jesus' character as a way of dismissing him; no matter how hard they tried, they couldn't get the healed man to back down from his story or to parrot the party line.

AFRAID OF THE RAMIFICATIONS

By now the interest of the whole community was piqued. The religious authorities refused to believe that a blind man had actually received sight, so they called in his parents for an "interview." But the parents knew better. They knew this was really an interrogation and that those asking the questions were not really seeking the truth. The whole community was colluding now to protect the status quo and to avoid having to confront what was beyond the limits of their own knowledge and experience.

The healed man's parents were common folk, the defenseless poor who were simply trying to survive in a religious system that was oppressive, punishing and at times even exploitive. When the Pharisees called them to testify about what had taken place, they were afraid, and rightly so. They *had* seen and they *knew* what was real, but they were afraid to answer truthfully for fear of punishment and expulsion from the spiritual community that was their very lifeblood. So when the Pharisees asked, "Is this your son, who you say was born blind? How then does he see?" they said, "Yes, he is our son. Yes, he was born blind. But how is it that he now sees? We can't answer that on grounds that might incriminate us. Ask him; he is of age. He will speak for himself."

The parents' fear was not a figment of overactive imaginations; they answered this way "because the Jews had already agreed that anyone who confessed Jesus to be the Messiah would be put out of the synagogue" (Jn 9:22). They knew that even though the Pharisees acted like they were asking a real question and seeking the truth, they were really just setting a trap. They had already decided who Jesus was—and who he wasn't. They had already agreed on the limits of what they were willing to see and know. Anyone who challenged what they already thought they knew would be put out. They did not want to be bothered with the facts, which left the parents needing to tap dance around the truth as best they could. On a day that should have been one of the happiest of their lives, they were afraid to name and celebrate the work of God in their family.

This is how paradigms, systems of thought, rigidly held categories and unquestioning loyalty to systems function. On the one hand, they help make sense of our lives so that we can function. But on the other hand, they have a powerful tendency to filter out any new information—including anything new God might be doing. They can filter out God himself!

A TALE OF TWO JOURNEYS

Meanwhile, the healed man was having his own experience. He was on a journey from blindness to sight on multiple levels. The healing of his physical sight happened in a moment, but the *real* journey—the journey from *spiritual* blindness to *spiritual* sight—gradually unfolded in the story. While everyone around him was asking all the wrong questions, arguing, posturing, maneuvering and trying to trip each other up, the healed man was on a journey of increasing spiritual insight into who Jesus really is. The light of the world was dawning in the man's heart:

- Early in the story he calls Jesus a "man" (v. 11).
- Then he calls him a "prophet" (v. 17).
- Then a "man . . . from God" (v. 33).
- Then Jesus calls himself the Son of Man (v. 35) and the blind man makes a full confession of faith, saying "'Lord, I believe.' And he worshiped him" (v. 38).

Now *that's* a good journey! The only problem is that it gets him thrown out of the religious community because the religious leaders were not on the same journey; they were moving in the opposite direction, descending further and further into spiritual darkness. Afraid to face their own inner darkness, their spiritual powerlessness, their lack of true knowing, they remained firmly entrenched in the outer darkness of their religious system. They neither recognized nor were ready to welcome the light of the world shining in their midst. Infuriated by a situation they could not control, they drove the blind man out.

The power to "drive someone out"—to dismiss, to denigrate and undermine what a person brings, in one way or another—is a power that we as leaders have. We can use that power irresponsibly when we are faced with truth that is unpleasant, inconvenient or challenges us in some way. Because of our place in the system, we can shut someone down or drive a person out without even being conscious of what we are doing or why we are doing it. Even if we *are* conscious of what we are doing, we can come up with ways to rationalize it—which the Pharisees probably did. We can even surround ourselves with those who are blind in the same ways we are, so we get caught up in the power of groupthink and cannot see things differently. When groupthink takes over in a leadership setting, we all miss the work of God. But since we have done it together, we have no idea that we missed it and might even congratulate ourselves on our excellent leadership!

The healed man in this story, however, stays quietly faithful to his own spiritual journey. He is learning that there is a powerful difference between belonging to a group and belonging to God. It is easier to try to fit in with the group than to be true to what you know. When we have encountered Christ's healing presence in ways that do not fit existing paradigms, we might find ourselves on the outside. That's the bad news.

It is easier to belong to a group than to belong to God. . . . Group-think is a substitute for God-think—[it is] the belief that God is found only by our group. The next step is to establish that identification with our group as the only way to serve God.

RICHARD ROHR, *EVERYTHING BELONGS*

MAKING SENSE OF IT ALL

The good news is that even though the healed man lost his place in the group, *he found Jesus*—or to be more accurate, *Jesus found him*—which is one of the most beautiful parts of the story. When Jesus heard that the Jews had driven him out of their community, he went to find the man. This was a great kindness because even though this man had been given the gift of restored sight, his good fortune and his spiritual clarity had now isolated him. He needed to understand what had happened and where he stood in relation to the community he had been a part of all his life. He needed to understand why, on this miraculous day, he found himself outside the religious community for being honest about what had happened to him.

While finding oneself on the outside can be traumatic at first, the healed man discovered it can also be a place of encounter. Away from the soul-numbing clamor of the religious community and all the ways they wanted to interpret and manipulate his experience, the healed man was finally able to reflect on all that had happened to him. He was able to touch the ground of his being, name the truth of his own encounter with Jesus and clarify what it meant to him. And Jesus, who knew what an unsettling day it had been, was there to help him piece it all together and take him the rest of the way on his journey toward full faith. In fact, Jesus seemed to think that those who have been expelled in this way actually have a head start in understanding his message because they had been expelled from what was unreal anyway.[1]

"Do you believe in the Son of Man?" Jesus gently asked.

"And who is he, sir? Tell me, so that I may believe in him."

"You have seen him (such good news!), and the one speaking with you is he."

After such a long and wearying day, and after waiting so long for a place to rest his soul, the healed man simply and finally gave himself over to his deepest knowing. *"'Lord, I believe.' And he worshiped him."*

Then Jesus gave him one more gift—helping him to further interpret the events of this day. He said, "I have come into this world to give sight to the blind and to make blind those who see." It was pretty clear that the healed man was in the first category, but the Pharisees were more than a little concerned about where Jesus' comment put them in the whole scheme of things. "Surely we are not blind, are we?" To which Jesus replied, "You know, it would be better for you if you were. *If you were blind, you would not have sin. But now that you say, 'We see,' your sin remains."*

This is the punch line of the whole story: those who admit their blindness see. Those who are convinced that they see and stubbornly refuse to admit their need for healing will not be able to see anything new. They will not progress on the spiritual journey. This story shows us that true discernment has very humble beginnings. It starts with the admission that we are not all that good at seeing. It begins with acknowledging the fact that we are as blind as bats sometimes, and there are many obstacles we need to overcome. Discernment begins when we acknowledge the fact that we lack the wisdom we need and that without divine intervention, the best we can do is stumble around in the dark. Discernment begins when we are in touch with our blindness and are willing to cry out from that place, "My teacher, I want to see."

Personal Reflection

As you reflect on John 9, ask God to show you where in the story you are. Are you most like the disciples, the Pharisees, the neighbors, the parents or some combination? How does this manifest itself in your own personal discernment and in your leadership discernment? As you become aware of the obstacles that prevent you from seeing the works of God and joining God in his work, confess this to God. Listen for how God might be inviting you to move beyond your own obstacles to seeing—both personally and in your discernment with others in community.

WHAT JOURNEY ARE YOU ON?

The most important step a group of leaders can take in becoming a community for discernment is to make sure that each individual is on the journey from spiritual blindness to spiritual sight. Since these obstacles function mostly at an unconscious level, if individuals in the leadership group are not on an intentional journey of transformation in which God is clearing away the debris, it won't matter what kind of process we have in place or what kind of verbiage we use about discerning and doing the will of God. It won't matter how intelligent the leaders are, how much theological education they have or how much business acumen they possess. The obstacles will prevent them from seeing the work of God that is unfolding right in front of their eyes.

Spiritual discernment is given to those who are spiritual, the Scriptures tell us, and those who are spiritual discern all things (1 Cor 2:12-16). Therefore, the most important prerequisite for discernment at the leadership level is that everyone in the leadership group is on an intentional journey of transformation—from spiritual blindness to spiritual sight. And Jesus is right there with us saying to each one of us, "I have come into this world so that those who do not see may see."

In Community

PRACTICING TOGETHER

John 9 is a profoundly disturbing passage for those of us who have been in and around institutionalized religion for a long time. And if we're honest, we probably find ourselves depicted somewhere in this story. As a group, share your thoughts on where you find yourself in this story and where you find yourselves as a group. Then discuss the following suggestions for moving beyond the obstacles you have identified:

- *If you identify with the disciples* and suspect that you might be asking the wrong questions and getting caught up in theological debates that miss the point, cultivate spiritual seeing by asking a different set of questions. Ask questions that have to do with healing rather than blame, loving real people in space and time rather than getting drawn in to theological arguments, noticing what God is up to and getting on board with that rather than being so intent on pushing your own agendas.

- *If you identify with the neighbors*, so stuck in your own paradigms that you can't see anything outside of them, ask God to reveal your paradigms for what they are—not necessarily bad, just limited. Ask God the brave question, Where are you bigger and more and outside of my way of thinking and constructing the world? If we are not willing to ask this question and see what God shows us in response, we end up with nothing more than the god of our own small minds!

- *If you identify with the Pharisees*, who were so caught up in preserving the system and their place in it that it became more important than what God was doing, get honest about it. All of us in leadership can probably find ourselves in this part of the story, at least to some extent. It takes great willingness, spiritual insight and self-awareness to notice where similar dynamics are at work in our own story. As we become more aware of this dynamic in ourselves, we might gently ask ourselves, What am I trying to protect? What do I stand to lose if I were to see—really see—what God is up to and sought to join him in it? Is this the place where God might be calling me to lose my life in order to gain "that which is life indeed"?

    These are brave questions, but remember: we have nothing to lose and everything to gain. All we have to lose is the false self and its attachments, which are illusions anyway. What we have to gain is the kingdom of God—that state of being in which God's will is being done *in our lives* as it is in heaven. This is life indeed.

- *We might even see a little bit of ourselves in the parents*—those who knew what they had seen but were afraid to say so because it would put them on the outside of the community they longed so desperately to be a part of. Sometimes "discerning the works of God" requires us to be willing to know what we know and work from there, regardless of the risk. They too wrestled with the reality that it is easier to belong to a group than to belong to God. It is easier to go along with the group than to know what you know and declare it when that is what's needed. Standing on the truth that you know may involve loss—like the loss of the perks that go along with being a part of a group. But how much better it is to live in the truth of what Jesus is actually doing in our lives and work from there!

As you close your group discussion, use the following prayer as a way of inviting God to remove the obstacles that prevent you from recognizing and responding to the activity of God in your midst.

CLOSING PRAYER
Heal our inner sight, O God,
that we may know the difference between good and evil.
Open our eyes
that we may see what is true and what is false.
Restore us to wisdom
that we may be well in our souls,
Restore us to wisdom
that we and our world may be well.[2]

2

BEGINNING WITH SPIRITUAL
TRANSFORMATION

Discernment in its fullness takes a practiced heart,
fine-tuned to hear the word of God and the single-mindedness
to follow that word in love. It is truly a gift from God,
but not one dropped from the skies fully formed.
It is a gift cultivated by a prayerful life
and the search for self-knowledge.

ERNEST LARKIN

∼

The leadership team of Grace Church wanted to learn how to discern God's will together as they made decisions. They were part of a large, well-established church in a busy suburb of a major city in the Pacific Northwest, and they had a passion for becoming a gathering place for spiritual seekers. And their vision had become reality! They had been able to assemble a top-notch team of individuals who were gifted and experienced in ministry, and they wore cool jeans. Most did not have any formal theological training, but they had innovative ideas, bright minds and a passion for Christ; through a variety of life experiences and marketplace opportunities, they knew how to develop and market their ideas effectively and implement them with excellence.

The elder board comprised leaders experienced at running successful businesses through good strategic planning processes and sound financial practices. There was also an attorney in the mix to make sure they always had good legal counsel, plus a brilliant strategist who had come to Christ through the church and was brimming with ideas about how to "take it to the next level." Since these individuals were well-connected and successful in their careers, they also had the funds to back whatever plans and visions they agreed on. They found it deeply fulfilling to be able to connect their financial successes with the opportunity to help fund such a significant spiritual endeavor. What had started out as a small group of families with a shared vision had now mushroomed to around two thousand in attendance on Sundays. In addition, many in the local community were benefitting from their wide array of ministries. They had been able to purchase a large warehouse, which they had renovated into a multipurpose space used for worship as well as for housing the many ministries that kept the place bustling with kingdom activity seven days a week. On the surface, it was all good.

Beneath the surface, however, there were other realities that needed attention. The staff was exhausted from continually trying to meet the needs of the community in ways that were bigger and better. There had been a moral failure involving one of the founding members, and although appropriate disciplinary action had been taken, there had not been open communication with those close to the situation. He and his family left the church abruptly, and many were still grieving the loss of their friend and colleague.

In addition, there had recently been a disagreement among the elders about purchasing a piece of property and expanding the ministry. This had created two factions in the congregation, one of which eventually left, bought the property and started another church several miles away. Public statements about how this would "expand the work of the kingdom" did little to heal the disillusionment among those who had been caught in the relational crossfire.

There were also stress cracks between the elders and the staff as relationships became increasingly hierarchical and businesslike. The staff felt that the elders wanted to see more bottom-line growth (attendance, offerings, new and innovative programs), but they weren't convinced that the elders really knew what it took to pull this off. The elders were now asking whether they had "the right people on the bus." Staff members were aware of conversations in which people's leadership "capacity" was questioned, and they feared being fired.

The senior pastor, the only staff person who was also an elder, carried the weight of being the one who continually represented the two groups to each other; this often resulted in miscommunication and misunderstanding. Several staff marriages were troubled due to pace of life issues and unresolved tensions. Those who were observant noticed that these couples attended fewer and fewer events, and when they did, they were aloof and guarded.

All of these dynamics created a prevailing mood of fear and uncertainty. Although staff and elders rarely got together as a group, the interactions they did have were characterized by posturing and maneuvering. Things were still going well externally, but there were aspects of the church's life where real wisdom was needed. How were they to discern what the real issues were, let alone God's will regarding them?

WHEN HUMAN WISDOM ISN'T ENOUGH

This is one kind of situation in which a leadership group might realize that they have reached the limit of what human wisdom has to offer and acknowledge their need for discernment. Something is not quite right. There is a realization that the methods they have used to make decisions in the past are not adequate for what they are facing now. Everyone is running so hard and so fast that no one has time or space to listen to God. They realize that even though they might have discerned God's will in the beginning, and that was how the whole venture got started, along the way something shifted. As things got larger and more complicated (or remained small and still became complicated!), they relied more on the wisdom of "experts" than on a mutual commitment to discern and do the will of God together. They might even have elevated leaders who were wise by human standards but were ill-prepared for spiritual discernment.

It could also be that everything in a church or organization is just right, and yet their leadership group is facing important and far-reaching decisions—such as an expansion of the physical plant, adapting a multisite strategy or making an important new hire—that require discernment rather than their own thinking and planning. How does a group of leaders discern God's will together on such matters?

BEGINNING AT THE BEGINNING

Leaders are often a bit surprised when I tell them where we need to begin. They usually have the idea that there is some sort of a technique I can teach in a weekend that will send them off and running. But what I tell them is that *corporate discernment begins with attending to the spiritual formation of each individual leader.* We start with the book of Romans, which contains Paul's clearest instruction that we are to "be transformed" so we can discern the will of God. We note that this passage was not addressed primarily to individuals but to a *group* of Christians who needed basic teaching about the Christian faith and how it is to be lived out. Romans 12–15, in particular, is focused on how we are to live out our faith in practical ways with each other in community, and it is in this context that Paul says: "In order for this thing called the body of Christ to work, each of you must resist the process of being conformed to this world and enter into a process of spiritual transformation so that together you can discern and do the will of God" (my paraphrase).

Groups determined to pursue God's will together must begin by focusing on the dynamic of spiritual transformation in the lives of individuals who comprise the group. The temptation, of course, is to skip the necessary prework and get on with the business of discernment. No doubt some groups will try to do this. Not to worry; some lessons are best learned the hard way. A group's initial attempts at discernment can actually clarify the need to enter into a more intentional process of spiritual transformation as they encounter their first obstacles or experience the limits of their spiritual readiness.

A group might start out strong but get stuck when they discover that while the individuals involved are intelligent and committed Christians, they do not have the spiritual practices in place that enable them to stay open to God in the context of a discernment process with others. Or when the discernment process becomes more difficult than they expected, they might observe people capitulating to what is worst within them—bullying, powering up, resorting to subtle manipulations, shading the truth, leaving in a huff and so forth.

Even then these initial failed attempts at discernment are fruitful because they help us *experience* the fact that spiritual transformation is indeed the necessary preparation for discernment. Failed attempts at discernment can provide the needed impetus to give focus to the spiritual formation of the leaders.

Discernment at the leadership level begins, then, with the spiritual transformation of each leader as they engage the disciplines that enable them to regularly offer themselves—body and soul—to God.

SPIRITUAL PRACTICES FOR DISCERNING LEADERS
Given the importance of spiritual transformation as a prerequisite

for discernment, it can be helpful for the leadership group to share an understanding of the process of spiritual transformation and how it takes place so they can all be on the same journey. (For a biblical and theological perspective on spiritual transformation, see appendix one.) There is no shortcut for this. Those who want to become discerners must have some basic spiritual practices in place to keep them in a posture of willing surrender to God. Sharing some understanding of key spiritual disciplines is essential for leaders seeking to pursue God's will together.[1]

Solitude and silence. Solitude is the foundational discipline of the spiritual life; it is time set aside to give God our full and undivided attention. In solitude we withdraw from our lives in the company of others and pull back from our many distractions in order to give God complete access to our souls. Devoid of the normal interruptions, silence deepens the experience of solitude. It enables us to withdraw not only from the noise and distraction of the external world, but also the "noise" of the inner compulsions that drive us. In solitude and silence, we become quiet enough to hear a voice that is not our own. This is the Voice we most need to hear.

Spiritual leadership starts with listening for the one true Voice and learning to distinguish it from all the other voices that clamor for our attention. Unfortunately, many leaders today preach solitude better than they practice it. Ironically, the more we get involved in Christian leadership the more difficult it can be to carve out time for God and the more subtle our excuses become. Perhaps we think that being at church or being so involved in God's work can somehow take the place of time alone in God's presence. Perhaps we think that leading prayer meetings and praying publicly is the same thing as having a prayer life. Or perhaps we are convinced that our presence and action are so critical for God's work to go forward that everything will come to a grinding halt if we let go and let God and others handle things while we take time in God's presence.

Maybe we have even become so addicted to the noise, activity and performance-oriented drivenness that characterizes so much of the church today that we don't know who we would be if we stopped to listen and receive. We might even think that reading the latest *New York Times* bestseller or the latest blog on leadership is more important to our leadership than receiving a word from the Lord.

Whatever our reasons for avoiding solitude, leaders more than anyone need to stop the flow of our own words and ideas long enough for God to get a word in edgewise. We need time to cease striving. We need to know something at a different level than just our intellect. We need time to listen to the still, small voice that is qualitatively different than any other. We need to hear those things that cannot be taught by human wisdom but by the Spirit. We need concrete ways of giving up control—at least for a time— so that God can be more in control of our lives and our leadership. Without this kind of listening and presence to God, it is impossible to cultivate leadership that is distinctly spiritual.

Personal Reflection

What is your experience of solitude and silence these days? How are you experiencing God's transforming presence in the context of these key spiritual practices?[2]

Engaging the Scriptures for spiritual transformation. As we cease striving in times of solitude, we realize that there is a difference between reading the Scriptures for utilitarian purposes—such as gaining information, preparing a sermon or proving a point—and engaging the Scriptures for spiritual transformation. There is a difference between approaching Scripture with our own agenda in mind (no matter how worthwhile that agenda might be) and approaching Scripture in order to wait on

God for what he knows we need. There is a difference between knowing the biblical stories and finding *ourselves* in the story in a way that helps us make sense of our lives and know God's guidance for our next steps.

Silence is the best preparation for hearing from God through Scripture—whether we are alone or together. "There is a wonderful power of clarification, purification and concentration upon the essential thing in being quiet," Dietrich Bonhoeffer writes. "Silence before the Word leads to right hearing and thus also to right speaking of the Word of God at the right time. Much that is unnecessary remains unsaid. But the essential and the helpful thing can be said in a few words."[3]

One approach to Scripture that fosters this kind of openness and receptivity is *lectio divina*, an ancient method of reading Scripture developed by the desert mothers and fathers to allow God to address them directly through the biblical text. (For a brief description of lectio divina, see appendix three.) Another way of opening to God through Scripture is to practice "finding ourselves in the story" like we did in John 9. In this practice we imagine ourselves in the historical setting and then listen to the story, allowing God to show us where we are in the story and to interact with us in that place. Or a designated person can read a relevant Scripture or the lectionary passage for the day and invite the group to remain silent for a few moments to allow God to speak personally to each one before anyone comments on the passage.

Leaders who place themselves before the Scriptures in a way that allows God to speak to them personally are more disposed to hear from God in ways that affect their decision making when they are with others. Because they regularly open themselves to God in Scripture as part of their own private devotion, they welcome the opportunity to be open to Scripture in a leadership setting. They don't experience the group devotional time as a precursor to "getting down to business." Instead, they are comfortable with using various approaches to Scripture as a way of inviting God to "speak into" meeting agendas as the discussions unfold and decisions take place. Whatever practices we use, cultivating patterns of listening to God in Scripture alone and together is essential to the fabric of spiritual leadership.

Personal Reflection

What is your practice these days for engaging Scripture for spiritual transformation? How is God speaking to you through Scripture? What kinds of things is he saying?

Prayer. Discernment takes place in the context of friendship with God as it is cultivated through prayer. Prayer encompasses all the ways we communicate and commune with God. The further we travel on the spiritual journey, the more we discover that all of life is prayer and holds the potential for deepening our intimacy with God. That said, there are three kinds of prayer that are particularly pertinent to discernment. The first is the *prayer of quiet trust* described in Psalm 131. In this silent prayer we acknowledge our utter dependence *on* God and trust *in* God when things are "too great and too marvelous for me." This is the kind of quiet trust that we might observe in a young child who is content to just be with his or her mother after weaning. It is only as we learn the prayer of quiet trust in the face of our own personal questions and complexities that we can enter into this kind of prayer in a leadership setting.

Another kind of prayer that is associated specifically with discernment is the *prayer for indifference.* In this prayer we ask God to work in our hearts to make us indifferent to anything but the will of God. This kind of indifference and willingness was Mary's response when the angel came to her and told her that she would give birth to the Messiah. "Here am I, the servant of the Lord; let it be with me according to your word" (Lk 1:38). It was Jesus' prayer after he had struggled in the garden of Gethsemane: "Not my will but yours be done" (Lk 22:42). We will explore this prayer more fully in chapter three.

When we have come to a place of indifference, we are ready for the *prayer for wisdom:* "If any of you is lacking in wisdom, ask God, who gives to all generously and ungrudgingly, and it will be given you" (Jas 1:5). We often pray for wisdom while we are already attached to some outcome we think is best! Indifference is an important prerequisite to the prayer for wisdom precisely because the wisdom of God is the foolishness of the world. When we have become indifferent to our need to be seen as wise in the eyes of others, then we are ready to receive wisdom from God. It is essential that elders, staff and ministry leaders are personally *on the journey* to this kind of surrender to God as part of their spiritual preparation for leadership.

Personal Reflection

What is your experience of the different kinds of prayer described here? Which are new? Which ones are you already practicing? How is God working in your life through these prayer practices?

Self-knowledge and self-examination. Parker Palmer makes this very sobering statement about leadership: "A leader is a person who must take special responsibility for what's going on inside him/herself, inside his or her consciousness, lest the act of leadership create more harm than good."[4] This statement explains, at least in part, Paul's confession in Romans 7 that "when I want to do what is good, evil lies close at hand."

Certainly no one understood the dangers of unexamined leadership better than Paul. After all, as Saul he was zealously committed to doing what was wrong while believing he was doing what was right. Some of us are like that! If we are not growing in self-awareness through honest self-knowledge and self-examination, there is every possibility that our leadership may in the end do harm where we had hoped to do good.

Palmer observes that people rise to leadership in our society based on their extroversion, which means they have a tendency to ignore what is going on inside themselves. These leaders rise to power by operating very competently and effectively in the external world, sometimes at the cost of internal awareness. He says, "I have met many leaders whose confidence in the external world is so high that they regard the inner life as illusory, as a waste of time, as a magical fantasy trip into a region that doesn't even exist. But the link between leadership and spirituality calls us to reexamine that denial of the inner life."[5]

The tendency to appoint leaders who have found success in the external world but who have somehow managed to ignore what is going on inside themselves is prevalent in the church and Christian organizations—especially in those that have grown large quickly. We assume that success in the world of business and commerce means a person is best qualified for leadership in the complicated environments of large churches and ministry organizations. While there is no question that great wisdom can be gained from experience in commerce, if spiritual preparedness is seen as secondary to skill, there will almost certainly come a time when that person's lack of self-knowledge and spiritual depth becomes a limiting (and even a debilitating) factor in his or her ability to provide spiritual leadership.

Gifted leaders—Christian or otherwise—can function effectively for a while on the basis of natural gifting and knowing how to maneuver in the business world. This does not necessarily qualify them for spiritual leadership. The destructive results of a lack of self-knowledge may not become evident until the person has been in leadership long enough for the public persona to fray around the edges when the pressure is on. When pushed against the wall, such leaders will capitulate to old, unresolved patterns.

Many leaders have been so shaped by work environments that are competitive, harsh and punitive that all they know to do is function in self-protective ways. When they become part of a spiritual community in which individuals are expected to be able to take responsibility for their mistakes, face their own character issues and confess their sin one to another in a way that fosters deeper levels of transformation, they honestly don't have the skills or spiritual capacity to do it. When spiritual leadership requires them to move beyond mere professionalism to "the more excellent way," they are not able to make the adjustment. They may even dismiss the call to grapple with issues of love, trust and transformation in a ministry setting as a lack of professionalism rather than seeing it as part of our calling to lead in ways that are distinctly Christian.

Personal Reflection

How do you practice self-examination these days? What is God revealing as you invite him to "search me and know me," as David did in Psalm 139? What is your awareness of the sin patterns, false-self motivations or character issues that might affect your leadership if they are not dealt with?

Discernment requires, first of all, that we are able to discern matters of our own heart. A leader cannot be discerning about external matters if they are not able to discern what is true and false within themselves. They become dangerous in the leadership setting because they are subject to hidden motives and defense mechanisms that are unknown even to themselves. In the preparation and selection of leaders, we need to look for those who are growing in self-awareness, who are willing to take responsibility for themselves and what drives their behaviors, *and* who have the courage to bring that self-knowledge into the leadership setting.

THE BEST THING YOU BRING TO LEADERSHIP

Just because an individual has been a Christian for a long time, attends church, went to a Christian college, has a Ph.D. in psychology or has been a leader in other settings does not mean that person is experiencing transformation at a level that will enable him or her to effectively engage in discernment with other leaders over the long haul. Just because people have natural gifts or share your passion for ministry does not ensure that they are practiced in the kind of prayer that leads to discernment. Just because they are successful businesspersons does not mean they are good at listening and responding to the still, small voice of God. Just because someone is a pastor or elder doesn't mean he or she can tell the difference between the true self and the false self, or is willing to die to what is false in order to respond to what is true and best. Being well-taught is not the same thing as being transformed.

The good news is that people can be shaped and educated within the group they are a part of, if they are willing. A group that understands itself to be a spiritual community that exists to pursue God's will together can and should, by its very nature, have a shaping influence on its members. In fact, this can (and should) be a stated goal of the group—to be a transforming community where this kind of formation for leadership can take place.

THE JOURNEY OF GRACE

With all of this in mind, the Grace Church leadership group decided to pause from adding any new ministry activities and spent six months focusing on their own spiritual lives. They wanted to move from decision making to discernment in their work together. They were convinced that their own transformation was prerequisite to this.

They began the process by creating space in a retreat setting for experiencing spiritual disciplines and listening to God together. They engaged a wise teacher to facilitate healing conversations about their pace of life, about how the relationships between staff and elders had deteriorated over the years, and about developing realistic expectations for people in ministry. They began to communicate openly, grieved past losses and brought some closure to the painful experiences that were part of their history.

As the retreat came to a close they were hopeful: they had released some very heavy burdens and were replenished and more aware of God's presence both personally and in community. But they didn't want this retreat experience to be a one-time mountaintop experience. They wanted this awareness of God's presence and the relational healing they experienced to be an ongoing reality, so they determined to spend the next six months reading about and practicing some basic spiritual disciplines. They agreed that the different ministry teams (including the elders) would devote at least part of their meetings once a month to sharing what they were experiencing in their spiritual practices. Six months later they would reconvene for another retreat in which they would be guided more specifically in the practice of discernment.

They were convinced that this attention to their own transformation as leaders was not a luxury or something they did when they had leftover time. It was the heartbeat of their shared life, and it was the only way to get on the path of pursuing God's will together.

In Community

PRACTICING TOGETHER

Take time as a group to reflect on the connection between spiritual transformation and discernment. Do you see it? Do you believe it? As a group, do you agree that spiritual transformation is a prerequisite to discernment?

Give time for each person in the leadership group to (1) talk about the spiritual rhythms they have in place, (2) how they are experiencing God in the midst of these rhythms and (3) what they still feel they need. Ask, What are the life rhythms that keep you healthy, growing and transforming? Have you established rhythms or patterns of spiritual practices that are shaping your spiritual lives *and* your collective leadership?

If everyone in the group is experienced in the spiritual disciplines described here and practicing them regularly, go on to chapter three. If some aren't, determine which disciplines the group needs to understand and practice more consistently. Then plan for a way to "get on the same page," either through reading and practicing on your own, scheduling a retreat for exploring the needed spiritual disciplines, or bringing in someone to teach or help guide the process. If the spiritual disciplines described here are relatively new to everyone, take time to study and experience some of the basic spiritual disciplines before going on. (If your group needs foundational teaching and experience with spiritual disciplines, *Sacred Rhythms* would be ideal, as it contains teaching, guidance for practicing each discipline and a group guide for processing your experiences together.) Another option is to identify the specific discipline(s) you need and take time between this meeting and the next to explore that one discipline. You might also consider using *Strengthening the Soul of Your Leadership*; it too connects spiritual practices with leadership specifically, and can serve as a helpful resource. Close your time by praying together.

CLOSING PRAYER
O God,
let something happen to me,
something more than interesting
or entertaining
or thoughtful.

O God,
let something essential happen to me,
something awesome,
something real,
Speak to my condition, Lord,
and change me somewhere inside where it matters,
a change that will burn and tremble and heal
and explode me into tears
or laughter
or love that throbs or screams
or keeps a terrible cleansing silence
and dares the dangerous deeds.
Let something happen in me
which is my real self, O God.[6]

3

LEADERS WHO ARE
DISCERNING

If you don't know how God is leading you,
you won't know how to lead others.

BYRON BRAZIER

❧

The focus on spiritual transformation had an immediate effect
on the leadership of Grace Church. Because new precedents had
been set at their retreat and through their practice of spiritual disciplines, the quality of their relationships began to change. They
viewed one another differently because they knew each other to
be people who were seeking God in intentional ways. Since the
staff and elders had decided together to take this step of valuing
their own process of transformation, the staff's fear of being fired
began to recede and there was more trust when they were together.
In meetings and other interactions, people found themselves more
readily taking responsibility for their own mistakes and bad behaviors, rather than blaming others for things that went wrong.

Even though there were still bumps in the relational road,

rather than being so reactive they took each situation into solitude to listen to God first. This led to a greater willingness to take responsibility for what went wrong and to process things together with more grace. Almost imperceptibly at first, they started to listen for God's promptings as they made their decisions. They were seeking to be responsive to God in their work and ministry. Thus they experienced more unity in the decisions they did make. Their pace of life became more sustainable because they were no longer adding new ministries until they went through a discernment process. They were more comfortable sharing what they were experiencing with God. And because they were growing in self-awareness, they started to understand the difference between being driven by their own plans and purposes and actually discerning and doing the will of God.

Although they didn't have words for it yet, something was changing. Ministry felt less stressful. And their relationships were becoming trustworthy enough that they felt comfortable opening up conversations about what God might want. Both staff and elders looked forward to reconvening to learn more about discernment. They were pretty sure that if they didn't know how to discern God's will for themselves, they would never be able to do it together as leaders in ministry. So they set aside a day to receive teaching and take the next step together.

A COMMON LEADERSHIP MISTAKE

We commonly assume that we can assemble a group of undiscerning individuals and expect them to be discerning leaders. Leaders of churches and Christian organizations are often successful in the secular marketplace, or even church ministry, but have had little instruction in or preparation for the process of discernment. They might not even understand discernment to be part of what they have been asked to do. In this kind of scenario, a Christian leadership team might be composed of:

- A successful investment banker who is very sincere and has a lot of money to contribute, but is such a young Christian that he barely knows what discernment is, let alone how to practice it in a leadership setting.

- An attorney whose approach to leadership is shaped more by her training as a lawyer than by any spiritual preparation.

- A construction company owner who was raised in the church his family helped plant. He stopped growing long ago and is committed to maintaining things "the way they've always been."

- An executive who climbed the corporate ladder by thinking strategically and learning how to "work the system." While he is a committed Christian and is enthusiastic about the mission of the organization, he relies primarily on his ability to think strategically. Since he came to faith fairly recently, there is very little integration of his business experience and practice with his spirituality. The idea that the wisdom of God is foolishness to this world is fairly incomprehensible.

- The pragmatist who has not yet had an experience of God that is beyond her own comprehension. She believes in the Holy Spirit *in theory* but is uncomfortable with the idea that the Spirit actually speaks to us today. In fact, she believes too much talk of the Spirit leads to mysticism.

Such individuals do have valuable gifts to bring to the leadership setting, and our churches and organizations would be impoverished without them. The problem, however, is when individuals bring *only* the training, experience and influences of a secular mindset without preparation in the areas of spiritual discernment. Without spiritual discernment it won't matter whether you have a clearly articulated discernment process, use Robert's Rules of Order or just offer perfunctory prayers to bookend your meetings—discernment is not going to happen! The people aren't right and they're not ready.

> There is no individual discernment outside a communal setting and no communal discernment without individual discernment. Each individual profits from the communal activity of discernment and the community profits from each individual's discernment.
>
> JOHN ENGLISH, *SPIRITUAL INTIMACY AND COMMUNITY*

FOUNDATIONS OF DISCERNMENT

While it is tempting to seek a technique that will enable a group like this to jump right to corporate discernment, it is a grave mistake to assume that these folks have a basic understanding of discernment or that they are practicing it as a way of life. The next step to becoming a leadership group that discerns God's will together is to cultivate a shared, working knowledge of the basics and to begin (or make sure people are) practicing discernment in their own lives. When even one person in the group is not habitually practicing discernment, it can derail the best attempts of the whole group.

Five foundational beliefs are the building blocks of a sound discernment practice. (If your group is knowledgeable and has had experience with discernment, feel free to skim these theological points and move on.) The first is that *spiritual discernment, by definition, is a process that takes place in and through the Trinity.* The Holy Spirit, the third person of the Trinity, "comprehends what is truly God's" and interprets the deep things of God to us (1 Cor 2:11-12). The Holy Spirit has been given to us by God, at Jesus' request, to lead us into truth (Jn 16:7-15). Commitment to discernment as a personal and communal way of life presupposes commitment to Christ *and* the real presence of the Holy Spirit, who has been given to lead and guide us on Christ's behalf. The Spirit is an immediate presence who can be heard and responded to through disciplines and practices that help us to listen.

Paul Anderson, professor of biblical and Quaker studies at George Fox University, makes this bold statement:

One great need of the church today is to experience the dynamic leadership of Christ as its Head. . . . The Scriptures promise us that Christ's Spirit will be with us, will guide us, and will lead us into all truth. This is the most striking implication of one's belief in the resurrected Lord. If Christ is alive he desires to lead his church. If Christ desires to lead his church, his will should be sought. If his will can be sought, it can be discerned; and if it can be discerned, it deserves to be obeyed. This is nothing more than the *basic Christian life*.[1]

The second building block is to *realize that the impulse to discern—to want to respond to Christ in this fashion—is in itself a "good spirit" that needs to be cultivated.* When individuals in a leadership group have a deepening desire to move beyond intellectual prowess and self-effort to spiritual discernment and all that it requires, this is evidence of the Holy Spirit's work among them. And this is pretty remarkable, because, as David Benner points out, even though we may desire to become more discerning,

> egocentricity and self-control are fundamental dynamics of the human condition. We know we are supposed to surrender to God's will and may genuinely want to, but most of us continue to face the almost irresistible tendency to assert our own will. We overhear Jesus' prayer in the garden of Gethsemane—"Not my will but thine be done"—but have trouble making it our own.[2]

This means that leaders who want to move into discernment mode have to rely on the Spirit to help them learn to distinguish between *willfully* asserting their own wishes (which can be cleverly disguised in so many different ways) to *willingly* surrendering to God's desires. They must learn how to submit to the work of the Spirit, who alone is able to transform our willfulness into willingness.

The third building block is *a deep belief in the goodness of God.* Any good Christian leader can wax eloquent about the goodness of

God; it is, after all, one of God's attributes. But many of us don't believe in God's goodness enough to trust God with the things that are most important to us. We may have suffered things for which we subtly blame God. Perhaps God disappointed us when we trusted him with something important. God's people have disappointed us. The process has disappointed us. Many of us are self-made people; we rely on ourselves and are proud of it. Truth be told, we don't really *want* to trust anyone but ourselves. How can we give ourselves to someone we're not sure will be good to us?

The only way we can freely participate in a discernment process is if we trust that God is good, not merely as a general attribute but as it relates to us specifically. Many of us will need to work at getting this building block set in the foundation of our discernment process. In order to surrender to the discernment process, we need to go beyond intellectual assent to cultivating a deep, experiential knowledge that God's will is the best thing that can happen to us under any circumstances. We need to hear God's voice whisper words of assurance to us, "I know the plans I have for you, plans for welfare and not for your harm" (Jer 29:11), and believe them in the depths of our being.

The fourth crucial building block for discernment is the conviction that *love is our ultimate calling—love for God, love of self, love for others and love for the world.* It is clear from Scripture that there is no other adequate measure of success for us as Christians (Mt 22:37-40; 1 Cor 13; 1 Jn 4:7-12). That we are to love God and others (including our enemies) is one thing we know for sure is the will of God!

This simple truth is easily lost in the press of church and organizational life. We rarely hear leaders ask what love might be calling them to do in the context of making major decisions. We can often detect a slow drift—imperceptible at first—from serving people to using them, from loving people to doing what is expedient, from being honest with them to spinning truth ever so slightly. By the time we notice how far we have drifted from this most basic aspect of God's will, we are in very dangerous waters!

The good news, of course, is that the Holy Spirit has been given to us to provide in-the-moment guidance for understanding the demands of love in the particularities of our situation. When seeking to discern God's will, it helps to keep before us the question of what love requires, and then create space for listening to what the Spirit says in response.

The fifth building block is that *we are committed to doing the will of God as it is revealed to us.* It does no good to discern the will of God if we are not committed to doing it—but sometimes that's the hardest part! Chuck Olsen and Danny Morris note,

> The question of willingness must be answered *before* the process of discernment begins: Are we willing to do God's will even before we know it? Or do we prefer to play games with God by saying, "God, show me your will and if I like it, I will do it." Spiritual discernment is not a game, and playing games with God leads to nothing but frustration.[3]

Jesus is very clear that "whoever does the will of God is my brother and sister and mother" (Mt 12:50; Mk 3:35). As we are faithful to discern and then actually *do* the will of God, we become the intimate family of Jesus.

Personal Reflection
How do you respond to the building blocks described here? Which of these building blocks is not firmly placed as a foundation for your own discernment? Is there anything else that would help you to wholeheartedly embrace discernment as a way of life?

DISCERNMENT AS A WAY OF LIFE
Discernment is much more than mere decision making; it is, first of all, a habit, a way of seeing that can permeate our whole life. As

we observed in John 9, it is the movement from seeing things merely from a human perspective to seeing from a spiritual vantage point, continually looking for evidence of the work of God in order to join him in it.

Discernment is a quality of attentiveness to God that, over time, develops into the ability to sense God's heart and purpose in any given moment. We become familiar with the tone, quality and content of God's voice. We notice how God is present for us in the moment. We wonder, *Where is God unfolding his work of love and redemption?* and *What is my most authentic response?*

> As important as the practices of discernment are, it would be improper to list them before the habit of discernment, because if the Holy Spirit has not been welcomed into the life of the discerner, practices of discernment will be empty and impotent. The habit of discernment constitutes a way of being, by which we are steeped in spirituality as a way of life . . . the habit of spirituality precedes the practices of discernment.[4]

Cultivating the habit of discernment means we are always seeking the movement of God's Spirit so we can abandon ourselves to it. Sometimes abandoning ourselves to the will of God is like floating down a river: we relax and allow the current of the river to carry us along. At other times it is more like trying to run the rapids or ride a large wave: we must keep our body and mind attuned to the dynamic of the water so we can ride it to its destination rather than being toppled by its force. Either way, we do not set the direction or the speed of the current; rather, we seek the best way to let the current carry us in the direction God has for us.

TESTING THE SPIRITS

Another crucial aspect of discernment is what Scripture calls "discernment of spirits" (1 Cor 12:10) or "test[ing] the spirits to see whether they are from God" (1 Jn 4:1). The discernment of spirits helps us to distinguish the real from the phony, the true from the false, in the external world but also in the interior world of our own thoughts and motives. As we become more attuned to these subtle spiritual dynamics, we are able to distinguish between what is good (that which moves us toward God and his calling upon our lives) and what is evil (that which draws us away from God).

Ignatius describes the inner dynamics of discerning the spirits as *consolation* and *desolation*. Consolation is the interior movement of the heart that gives us a deep sense of life-giving connection with God, others and our authentic self. We may experience it as a sense that all is right with the world, that we are free to be given over to God and love, even in moments of pain and crisis. Desolation is the loss of a sense of God's presence; indeed, we feel out of touch with God, with others and with our authentic self. It might be an experience of being off-center, full of turmoil, confusion and maybe even rebellion. Or we might sense our energy draining away, tension in our gut or tears welling in our eyes.

Consolation and desolation are not mere emotions. They are visceral, in-the-body experiences that precede emotion or affect, alerting us to truth that is sensed and known in the inward being before we are conscious of it.

For instance, you might be going through something very difficult—perhaps the death of someone close, or quitting a job or ending a relationship that is not good for you. There certainly is sadness or fear and concern about the future. But underneath these emotions, you might also identify a deep sense of well-being—"the peace that passes understanding," God's presence comforting or leading you. *This* is consolation.

It can go the other way as well. You might experience something that seems good to you or others—a promotion at work or an advantageous relationship. But deep inside you sense anxiety, *dis*-ease, dread. You sense that you will not be able to maintain the truest aspects of yourself. *This* is desolation. Your body knows and is telling you something your mind doesn't want to know or may not be ready to know yet.

This aspect of discernment, says Ernest Larkin,

> depends greatly on our spiritual and psychological maturity. If we are ambivalent and divided by chaotic emotions and neurotic conditions, our affective states will provide no positive guidance. Our task will be to understand our condition and bring order into our affective life. But as we come to achieve that discipline, in proportion as we die and our lives are hidden with Christ in God, discernment becomes more effective.[5]

CONSOLATION, DESOLATION AND LEADERSHIP

The habit of *personal* discernment establishes and cultivates the ability to pay attention to things many leaders are not accustomed to paying much attention to in a leadership setting. Over time personal discernment teaches us that there is something "inside" that we can trust enough to offer to the group in a leadership setting. As our own Transforming Center leadership community has grown in the practice discernment over the years, we have had many experiences of paying attention (or wishing we had paid more attention!) at this level and allowing it to inform our decision making.

There was a time very early in our leadership experience when we got together for a strategic planning day. We spent the day doing just that—coming up with all these great ideas that seemed very strategic. Our brilliant thoughts were written on newsprint that was taped on the walls for all to see. But all that brainstorming came from our heads. We neglected to pay attention to the subtle inner dynamics we were experiencing.

When the day was done, we all looked at the newsprint and no one had energy for any of it. No one volunteered to drive any of the initiatives or take up any of the tasks. I remember taking down the newsprint very carefully, folding it up very precisely, trying to

convince myself that if our board secretary went home and wrote
it all up, we would eventually do something with it.

We never did.

We probably still have that newsprint, but the plans never went
anywhere because we weren't paying attention and responding to
all levels of our knowing. Whatever experience we had in personal discernment, we weren't yet comfortable bringing it into the
leadership setting, and we paid a hefty price in a wasted day.

In a more recent example, I broached the possibility of purchasing
a facility we were all familiar with. When I brought it to the board for
consideration, one board member immediately said that even
thinking about embarking on the kind of fundraising that such a
purchase would require, and taking on the care and maintenance of
such a significant property during the current recession, made his
heart race. He even (unknowingly) clutched his chest as he was
speaking! He was not being melodramatic or manipulative; he was
being honest about a very clear experience of desolation. Because we
were accustomed to listening to one another in this way and knew
each other well enough to know that fear and an unwillingness to
take a risk were *not* this person's false-self patterns, it was easy for us
to listen to his experience, respect it and then respond.

In a very comfortable exchange, another board member shared
his own experience of leading his church through a capital campaign. He described how consuming the campaign had been for
the staff and how much organizational energy it took not only to
raise the funds but also to operate and maintain it after it was built.
We all resonated. Of course, a case could have been made that this
purchase was strategic and necessary for all sorts of good reasons.
We could have taken a couple hours to hear a presentation and
discuss it, but that conversation wasn't needed. God was already
speaking clearly through (in this case) an experience of desolation
in one of our respected leaders, and that was all we needed.

The willingness and the ability to pay attention to that place where God's Spirit is speaking to us deep within and to name it out loud actually simplified the conversation and created space for God to speak and guide us.

AN INVITATION TO CHOOSE LIFE

In Deuteronomy 30 God addresses the whole company of Israel through Moses and says, "I have set before you life and death, blessings and curses. Choose life so that you and your descendants may live." God's will for us is generally to do more of that which gives us life (Deut 30:11-20; Jn 10:10) and to turn away from those things that drain life from us. Furthermore, God points out that the wisdom that enables us to choose life is not something we will find outside of ourselves—in heaven or across the ocean— but that this knowing is very near to us; it is in our mouths and in our hearts for us to notice and observe (Deut 30:19-20).

In the New Testament Jesus says, "I have come that you might have life and have it abundantly" (Jn 10:10 ESV). Many of our smaller decisions and most of our significant decisions—even decisions that require us to choose between two equally good options—involve the ability to notice what brings a sense of life, freedom in the Spirit (2 Cor 3:17), the peace that passes understanding (Phil 4:7). These inner dynamics need not be attached to anything that is particularly momentous; in fact, they might *seem* relatively inconsequential until we learn to pay attention and trust what they have to tell us. That slight tension headache we get as we interact with a particular person or the aspect of our job that is inordinately draining, the life-giving energy we feel in the presence of art and beauty, the sensation of being "in the flow" when we are engaged in a particular activity, the feeling of peace we notice as we walk into a particular building or space—these are experiences of "life" and "death" that we can be attentive to and receive guidance from.

The opportunity to choose life is ours—in the day-to-day choices we face as well as in the larger decisions of our lives.

This opportunity is there for us in our personal decisions and in the leadership decisions that affect many others. When we make it our habit to notice and respond to that which is life-giving, we are in touch with what is truest about God, ourselves and our world. Then, when we are called upon to make larger decisions—even in the leadership setting—we can draw upon all of the understanding and awareness we are gaining to inform our decision.

Personal Reflection

Take a few moments to notice experiences of consolation and desolation over the last twenty-four hours. Ask God to reveal a moment you are most grateful for—a moment that was life-giving, energizing, when you were able to give and receive love, when you were your best self, when you felt connected with God. That is consolation. Then ask God to show you a moment for which you are least grateful—a moment that drained life and energy from you, when you were unable to give and receive love, when you were not able to be your best self or felt discon-nected with God. That is desolation. God invites us to choose life. As you reflect on these experiences, is there any wisdom or insight that comes about how you can choose life?

DYNAMICS OF DISCERNMENT

At some point we are faced with a decision that requires us to make a choice in which we are aware of our desire to discern the will of God in the matter. Now we discover that discernment is also a spiritual *practice* that does what all spiritual disciplines do: it offers us a concrete way of opening to the activity of God beyond what we can do for ourselves.

While it is beyond the scope of this book to outline the practice of personal discernment in detail, I will describe several dynamics of discernment that can be practiced personally in such a way as to prepare individuals for discernment at the leadership level.[6]

The prayer for indifference. The first and most essential dynamic of discernment is *the movement toward indifference*, which was referred to in chapter two. In the context of spiritual discernment, *indifference* is a positive term signifying that "I am indifferent to anything but God's will." This is "interior freedom" or a state of openness to God in which we are free from undue attachment to any particular outcome. There is a capacity to relinquish whatever might keep us from choosing God and love, and we have come to a place where we want God and God's will more than anything—more than ego gratification, more than wanting to look good in the eyes of others, more than personal ownership, comfort or advantage. We ask God to bring us to a place where we want "God's will, nothing more, nothing less, nothing else"[7] so that we can pray the prayer *of* indifference—"Not my will but thine be done."

Coming to a place of indifference is no small thing—especially if we are facing a decision in which the outcome really matters to us or we have a vested interest in it. It is even harder in a leadership setting where egos are on the line, where posturing and maneuvering is the norm and territorialism lies right under the surface of our polite prayers, words and handshakes. In fact, indifference is not something we can achieve for ourselves. Just like everything else that is of significance in the spiritual life, God must accomplish this for us—which is why all we can do is pray and wait for it to be given. And God cannot give us indifference apart from our offering ourselves to him in the discipline of detachment.[8]

A question that can help us identify where we need to be made indifferent is, What needs to die in me in order for God's will to come forth in my life? or, Is there anything I need to set aside so that I can be open to what God wants? There are times when the answer requires death to self so the life of Christ can be born more fully in us. It is a spiritual death in which we lay down our own will in order to embrace God's will.

When we know we are not indifferent and cannot accomplish indifference for ourselves, the prayer for indifference may take us into a period of waiting. All we can say to God is, "I know I am not indifferent. I know that part of me still clings to my own agenda. If I am to become indifferent, you will have to do it in me." This period of waiting may feel very dark. But strangely enough, it will also feel deeply right—like we are right where we need to be.

The prayer for wisdom. The movement toward indifference is the threshold between two worlds—the world of human decision making and the spiritual practice of discerning the divine will. In this waiting room of the soul we are made ready to pray the second prayer—the prayer for wisdom: "If any of you is lacking in wisdom, ask God, who gives to all generously and ungrudgingly, and it will be given you" (Jas 1:5). Since we have died to our need to be wise in others' eyes or to prove ourselves according to human standards, we are finally ready to ask for God's wisdom and receive it.

It is *crucial* that those of us who want to become more discerning learn to grapple with this part of the process—to be able to recognize places of unfreedom where we are inordinately attached to a particular outcome rather than being indifferent to anything but the will of God. This is mature spirituality, and we will not be able to lead from this place of self-awareness and openness to God in a leadership setting if we have not practiced in our personal lives.

Notice without judging. Another dynamic of discernment is the ability to *notice everything pertinent to the situation—both external and internal—without judging, at least at first.* Most of us are accustomed to observing the obvious as we make decisions—circumstances, the clear meaning of pertinent Scriptures, the advice of wise Christian friends and the wisdom contained in our faith tradition. These form the basic framework for our Christian living, and it is assumed that we are making decisions within this framework, especially at the leadership level. That is discernment 101.

The more complex the decisions facing us, the more we must move beyond the basics of discernment to considering inner dynamics, which are harder to notice and interpret. We learn to listen to the stirrings of desire, to distinguish our true, God-given desires and calling from externally imposed "oughts" and "shoulds" and the compulsions of the false self. We are willing to pay attention and give credence to consolation and desolation. These dynamics are much more subtle, yet they give us clues as to what choices will nurture the life of Christ lived in and through our most authentic selves.

In addition to paying attention to that which is conscious, discernment calls us to pay attention to any unconscious matter that comes up as well. It could be truth that slips out in honest conversation (before we have a chance to edit ourselves!) or that presents itself to us in dreams.

One of the things that always strikes me about the Christmas story is the prominence of the role of dreams. God was very active in communicating through dreams—with Joseph in particular. And Joseph was obedient in responding. If Joseph had ignored his dreams as unworthy of consideration, or if he had willfully refused to obey what he heard in those dreams, the Christmas story would have unfolded very differently.

There is nothing in Scripture to indicate that God has given up on speaking to us in dreams. In fact, in my work as a spiritual director I often encourage people to pay attention to their dreams because when we are asleep we are less ego-defended and more able to receive a prompting from God that is beyond what our cognitive faculties can accept. Of course the content of dreams and how we interpret them is still subject to other aspects of a disciplined discernment process, but they are worth paying attention to nonetheless.

All this to say, the will of God is manifest deep within, where the Spirit dwells and bears witness with our spirit about things that are true (Rom 8:16). A profound life orientation is revealed in our deepest desires and consolations, when we are able to get in touch with them. These usually have something to do with our calling—the very purpose for which God created us. This is a passion or a burden that is uniquely ours and cannot be set aside without doing damage to ourselves and to our relationship with the One who has called us. This is true for churches and ministries as well. Discerning leaders stay in touch with the calling and charisms of the community they are leading, learning to be humbly confident in making decisions consistent with who God has called them to be—as individuals and as a group.

Deep within us all there is an amazing inner sanctuary of the soul, a holy place, a Divine Center, a speaking Voice, to which we may continuously return. Eternity is at our hearts, pressing upon our time-torn lives, warming us with intimations of an astounding destiny, calling us home unto itself. Yielding to these persuasions, gladly committing ourselves in body and soul, utterly and completely, to the Light Within, is the beginning of true life.

Thomas Kelly, *A Testament of Devotion*

Seek spiritual direction and greater discernment of spirits. This is a good place to mention that spiritual direction is a key component to a lifestyle of discernment for leaders. It is tempting to think that once we have done a little reading on discernment and once we have practiced a bit, we don't need any help with discernment, but this is just not true. In fact, there is an even greater need for spiritual direction as we progress in the spiritual life. So far we have only referred to content found in the "first set of rules" Ignatius outlined for understanding consolation and desolation, but there is a second set of rules "for greater discernment in the second spiritual situation."

Ignatius describes the second spiritual situation as a time when the evil one uses a new tactic—"deceptive spiritual consolation that is not of the good spirit and [that] will lead, if followed, to spiritual harm"—in his efforts to deceive mature Christ-followers.[9]

Father Tim Gallagher describes the second spiritual situation this way: "A point may come on the spiritual journey when persons who deeply love God must be aware of, understand, and reject certain attractions toward good and holy things that, if undertaken, would distract from different good and holy things to which God is genuinely calling them. . . . Holiness of life, even great holiness of life, does not eliminate the need for discernment of spirits; rather, it is precisely goodness of life that calls for the greater discernment of spirits found in Ignatius' second set of rules."[10] Gallagher goes on to say that spiritual direction is most needed at this time: "Ignatius presumes that dedicated persons will find real discernment in such times with the help of a competent spiritual guide. He envisages such spiritual accompaniment as a constant in all discernment of spirits and most especially in connection with the 'second spiritual situation' in which we experience 'temptation under the appearance of good' through spiritual consolation."[11]

Most leaders who find themselves in leadership in a church or Christian organization are clearly in the "second spiritual situation," in which it is perilous to engage in discernment without wise spiritual direction. At the very least we need a wise spiritual friend in whose presence all inner dynamics can be attended to without bias. As Thomas Merton so wisely states, "[The spiritual director's] function is to verify and encourage what is truly spiritual in the soul. He must teach others to 'discern' between good and evil tendencies, to distinguish the inspirations of the spirit of evil from those of the Holy Spirit. A spiritual director is, then, one who helps another to recognize and to follow the inspirations of grace in his life, in order to arrive at the end to which God is leading him."[12]

It is ironic that sometimes, as we progress in the spiritual journey, we convince ourselves that we are beyond needing spiritual guidance, when in reality, that is actually the time when the evil one switches tactics and we need spiritual counsel more than ever.

Gather and assess information. Another dynamic of discernment is the ability to *ask good questions and to allow those questions to help us gather data and gain perspective.* These are not necessarily questions that will get us the answers we want; rather, they are questions that will elicit the deeper wisdom we need. A good question has the power to throw open a door or a window so that a fresh wind of the Spirit can blow through.

There are many questions that help us reflect spiritually on the objective facts and also gain insight into the deeper dynamics of the situation. At different times, different questions will resonate and help us attend to the different ways God's will is manifest in and through our circumstances and in the inner, spiritual dynamics that are present. The following are some questions that leaders who want to become more discerning can learn how to ask and reflect upon honestly. The experience of interacting with such questions in more personal matters prepares us to frame better questions at the leadership table and to reflect on them honestly with others as well.

- *Direction and calling.* How does this choice fit with the overall direction and calling of God on my life? Is there a word or phrase that captures my sense of calling these days, and will this choice enable me to continue living into my calling?

- *Consolation and desolation.* Which choice brings the deepest sense of life, inner peace and freedom (Jn 10:10; Phil 4:7; 2 Cor 3:17)? As I consider moving in this particular direction, is there a growing sense of wholeness, authenticity and congruence with who I am in God?

- *Desire.* What is my deepest and most authentic desire relative to the choice I am facing? What is my response when Jesus asks, "What do you want me to do for you? What is it you seek?"

- *Scripture.* Is there a particular Scripture that God is bringing to mind relative to this choice? What is it saying to me?

- *Life of Christ.* Is this choice consistent with what I know about the mind and heart of Christ and his loving, redemptive purposes in the world?

- *Character growth and development.* What is God doing in my character and spiritual growth, and will this choice continue to nurture this growth? How will this direction nurture the fruit of the Spirit in me—particularly the fruit of love, which is at the heart of our Christian calling and the litmus test for what it means to be truly Christian.

- *Love.* Given the primacy of love and unity in Christ's teachings, what does love call for in this situation?

- *Clarify perspective.* It's hard to see the whole field when we are mired in the details. Take a step back to look at the larger patterns of what God is doing in your life. Which choice fits the larger patterns that are already in motion? Take a step forward—to your deathbed. If I imagine myself on my deathbed, which choice would I wish I had made? Does this choice value what is eternal and permanent, what holds the deepest value, rather than what is transient and impermanent?

- *Community.* How does this choice fit with others' observations of who I am and what God is doing in my life? Am I willing to open up every facet of this decision to a trusted spiritual friend or director for their wisdom and insight? Is there anything in the overall tradition of the Christian faith that might inform my decision?

Personal Reflection

Which question is most compelling or most helpful relative to a decision you are facing?

Cultivate solitude as a time for listening to God around these and similar questions. Jesus himself set aside times of solitude for intense prayer and listening at important choice points in his life. The very beginnings of his public ministry came as a result of listening to the voice of his Father affirm his identity as the beloved Son (Mt 3:13-17). Matthew 4 describes how he was driven into the wilderness to struggle with subtle temptations regarding his calling. In Luke 6 we observe Jesus' choice to spend the night alone in prayer before making his decision about who he would choose as his disciples—certainly one of the most important decisions of his life in ministry. Luke 22 describes another night spent in solitude, when Jesus struggled mightily with his calling to go to the cross; he did not stop until he had wrestled all the way through it and was ready to do the will of God.

Since Jesus, who was already so intimate with God, felt the need for solitude relative to discerning and doing God's will, it is certain that we need it as well. We only want people at the leadership table who practice solitude and silence as a place for hearing God's voice relative to decisions they face and who are open to incorporating this into their leadership discernment as well.

Identify and work with options. At some point in the discernment process a way forward starts to become clear. There may even be a couple of options that seem equally good. Go ahead and identify those as clearly as possible and even improve them or combine them into one option that combines the best of both.

Now God invites us to make a choice—at least privately—and to once again rely on the inner experience of consolation and desolation by *seeking inner confirmation.* We can take some time to live with our choice privately and see whether there is a sense of rightness about it, a sense of being in harmony with oneself— the person God created me to be and I want to be. We can take several days to walk around as if we have made a certain decision and notice where there is the greatest level of life and sustaining energy. (If there are two equally good options, walk around for a few days as if you have made one decision, and then do the same for the other.)

While you are walking around as if you've made one decision or the other, notice, What is the truest and most authentic expression of the Spirit in and through my life *at this time?* It is important to be able to recognize where this peace and consolation rests. Is the ego part of me at peace because I am choosing something that will keep the ego in control? Is the fearful part of me at peace because I am choosing a path that keeps me safe and secure? Or does this peace reside in the deepest, truest part of me—the part that has the capacity and willingness to be completely given over to God?

Do not let yourself get pushed to make a decision until you have had the opportunity to do this. The restraint that individuals learn to practice in their personal lives pays off when the pressure to rush things along becomes intense in the leadership setting.

Abandoning ourselves to God. Ultimately, discernment is about being completely given over to God in love and allowing that love to guide everything. It is about knowing God so intimately that we can tell what he wants just by turning our hearts toward him. It is about trusting God so much that all we want in this life is to abandon ourselves to the goodness of God's will. It is about valuing God's will so much that we will wait until we feel we have discerned God's will before taking action.

This presumes a great deal of experience with the dynamics of discernment—that we are allowing God to purify our desires, dismantle the false self and draw us into the kind of intimacy that puts us in touch with what is truest within. It presumes a willingness to submit to the most penetrating questions, testing all decisions to see if they square with our experience of being "at home" in God, where we are living in total surrender to that ultimate goodness we have come to know and trust. It requires absolute commitment to doing the will of God even before we know what it is. It is here that we prove ourselves faithful in the smaller things of our own lives so that God can entrust us with the "much" of leadership. This kind of leader is the *only* kind you want on the "bus" that everyone has decided to ride—the "bus" of pursuing the will of God together.

CONTINUING THE JOURNEY

The leadership group at Grace Church was excited about the day they spent exploring the dynamics of personal discernment together. They were surprised to discover that they had never given much thought to what they believed about discernment, and they were unfamiliar with some of the dynamics associated with it.

The biblical idea that discernment is an invitation to choose life was a welcome revelation. And they were surprised by the fact that exploring these things together deepened their sense of community with each other. The simple practice of sharing their experiences of consolation and desolation had opened new levels of sharing. This gave them a renewed hope for what their life together in ministry could be. Excited about exploring the dynamics of personal discernment over the next few months, they felt for the first time that they were on the right bus.

The plan was that each would choose one or two other people from the group to share with as they went. These spiritual companions would meet every two weeks to notice consolation and desolation (along the lines of the personal reflection at the end of the section "An Invitation to Choose Life" in this chapter), and to share aspects of the discernment process they were in. The idea of cultivating this kind of spiritual companionship within their ministry context was a new frontier, but they were willing and enthusiastic. They were taking their first steps to becoming a community that could discern God's will together.

In Community

PRACTICING TOGETHER

Take time as a group to share from your reflections on the founda-tions and dynamics of discernment. Which were new for you? Which felt somewhat familiar? Where did you resonate and where did you resist?

If the group feels safe enough, invite individuals to share an area in their lives where they are seeking discernment. What aspect of this chapter was most helpful in actually discerning God's will in regard to your question for discernment?

CLOSING PRAYER

Lord,
I believe my life is touched by you,
that you want something for me
and of me.
Give me ears
to hear you,
eyes
to see the tracing of your finger,
and a heart
quickened by the motions
of your Spirit.
Amen.[13]

4

COMMUNITY AT THE
LEADERSHIP LEVEL

*The spiritual radiation of a community depends on
the commitment of its members to the transformational journey
and to each other. To offer one another space in which to grow
is an integral part of this commitment.*

THOMAS KEATING

∂∞

Their leadership of Grace Church reconvened a few months later for a follow-up retreat in which they would learn more about the specifics of becoming a community for discernment. Enthusiasm was high. These times of learning and conversation had become a safe place to talk about important matters, and the leaders always came away feeling spiritually enriched. They were already experiencing a deepening of their relationships in community and were curious about what else they could do to foster this reality in their leadership setting.

Their facilitator began by reflecting on what the last few months had been like—in their relationships with God and with each other. They observed that they felt more alive spiritually as they paid attention to consolation and desolation. The presence of God seemed more real and immediate. They also noticed that their relationships with each other were becoming more substantive because of the conversations they were having about their personal experiences of discernment.

Sometimes they even referred to the dynamics of discernment in discussions about the decisions they were making together. They were able to talk about things like indifference, consolation and desolation. And though they didn't always know what to do in response to these discussions, being able to talk about them with shared language and understanding seemed honest and respectful.

One person reported that she used a couple of the questions for personal discernment in the context of a meeting where an important decision was being made, and the questions helped clarify the way ahead for the whole group. Another shared about a personal interaction with another staff member when things had gotten tense and opinions were stated a bit too strongly. He remembered the prayer of quiet trust and discovered that quieting himself in God's presence and returning to a place of trust in God rather than going with his first reaction (as he was prone to do) helped him to respond more gently. Somehow this gentle response diffused the situation and allowed them to move forward in a more productive way.

As the staff and elders shared, their excitement grew. How was it that this focus on personal spiritual disciplines and discernment was making a profound impact on the group? Why hadn't they learned this long ago? What could they do to further this experience of transforming community so they could be even more intentional about discerning and doing God's will together? Stumbling into moments of discernment was great, but they were hungry to see it happen more regularly. They were honest enough to acknowledge a feeling of vulnerability as well. They recognized that they were sharing more of themselves with each other than they had before; it was good but also very different than the businesslike (and slightly self-protective) demeanor they were used to. They kept wondering, *How far can we go with this? Where will it take us? And is it really safe?*

BEYOND TEAMWORK

Those of us who were thinking about leadership in the 1970s and 1980s were inspired—and rightly so—by the concept and wisdom of teams. If you have ever had the privilege of living in a city that boasts an award-winning sports team (like the Chicago Bulls in their day), you know that effective teamwork yields great entertainment and great results!

But as inspiring as the idea and the reality of teamwork is, it falls short of what Christians are called to be. Those of us who come together to lead churches and organizations with a Christian purpose answer to a deeper calling: to move *beyond* teamwork and *live into* that great spiritual reality called Christian community. A New Testament perspective makes it clear that Christian community is made of people who gather around the transforming presence of Christ so they can do the will of God (Mk 3:34-35). Jesus didn't choose a high-powered board or even a winning team to spearhead what would eventually become a worldwide movement. He chose to live with his disciples in an intimate expression of transforming community so that their ministry and their leadership could emerge from there.

The community of Jesus is not a human reality that we create but a spiritual reality that already exists in Christ. As Dietrich Bonhoeffer points out,

> It is a gift of God that we cannot claim. It is not an ideal which we must realize; it is rather a reality created by God in which we may participate. . . . Because Christian community is founded solely on Jesus Christ, it is a spiritual and not a psychic reality. In this it differs absolutely from other communities.[1]

THE NATURE OF SPIRITUAL COMMUNITY

One of the fundamental differences between a team and a spiritual community is that a team assembles around a task and is bound together by a commitment to that task. Whether the task is winning basketball games, building Habitat for Humanity houses or founding a church, when the task is over, things get difficult or a better offer comes along, people feel free to leave or the team disbands. Spiritual community, on the other hand, gathers around a Person—the person of Christ present with us through the Holy Spirit.

The root meaning of *community* is to "come together" in "unity." The word *community* comes from *communis*, meaning "common," and from *communicare*, meaning "to share or participate." People can come together in unity around many things; they can participate together in a variety of common causes. What makes a community distinctly spiritual is that we gather around the presence of Christ, mediated through the Holy Spirit. We are unified by our commitment to be transformed in Christ's presence through the work of the Holy Spirit so we can discern and do the will of God as we are guided by the Spirit. We participate in Jesus' prayer "Thy kingdom come; thy will be done" in our own small corner of the world.

Since spiritual transformation results in the ability to discern God's will, mission often emerges when Christians gather—whether we intended it to or not! In relationship with Jesus, we are naturally drawn into Jesus' redemptive and loving purposes in the world. But whatever mission we are called to needs to *grow out of* and *remain grounded in* the commitment to continually gather around the transforming presence of Christ and to listen for his direction in our lives. This is spiritual community as Jesus defined it: "Here are my mother and brothers! Whoever does the will of God is my brother and sister and mother" (Mk 3:34-35).

CONVERSION TO COMMUNITY

Jesuit priest and spiritual director John English notes that one of the many contributions of Ignatius Loyola in the sixteenth century was to "promote faith communities that image themselves as gatherings to discern the presence of Christ everywhere. The emphasis is on recognizing what is happening, so as to follow the lead of the Spirit in the context of the whole life of humankind."[2] This is a major shift in a group that involves

> some form of conversion to the significance of community . . . so that eventually, the image of the community becomes that of a discerning apostolic group. Such a community realizes its identity as an experience of the risen Christ in its midst. . . .
>
> This identity calls forth a sense of unity and responsibility to the Holy Spirit's activity within and beyond it to the benefit of all humanity. The community accepts that the Trinity is active in our lives, constantly creating, healing, freeing, encouraging, calling us forth, uniting with us in sorrows and joys, in trials and triumphs, in good times and bad times. But we look for this action in a communal way rather than in an individualistic way.[3]

This is a very big statement, but it is true. When a leadership group moves from seeing itself primarily as a board or a leadership team to defining itself as a spiritual community, it does constitute something of a conversion. Like all conversions it will involve turning away from old thought patterns in order to embrace new ones. It may involve embracing a new set of values (or old values that somehow got lost) while at times minimizing or setting aside things we have previously valued. It will involve orienting ourselves to a new set of priorities and practices, and reallocating time to those priorities. And it involves a deeper level of commitment to each other that extends far beyond the task at hand.

In most cases, it is unwise to move to the nuts and bolts of leadership discernment until this "conversion to community" has taken place. Or if you have the opportunity to assemble a leadership group around a new cause or a mission, it is best to start out by clearly defining the group as a community for discernment and invite only those who are willing to participate at that level. The presence of even one person who doesn't get it or who actively resists—no matter how gifted he or she might be in other ways—can negatively affect a group's ability to function well as a spiritual community.

> ### *Personal Reflection*
>
> *How do you respond to the idea of moving beyond teamwork to spiritual community in your current leadership group? Pay attention to resonance and resistance. Even (and perhaps most especially) if you feel resistant, don't judge yourself but rather be curious about why you are resisting and where that resistance is coming from. Talk to God about it or write about it in your journal.*

BECOMING A TRANSFORMING COMMUNITY

For some reason it is much easier to talk about community and even try to create community for others than it is to actually *be* a community at the leadership level. There are many reasons for this—not the least of which is that it takes a lot more work, intentionality, vulnerability and openness to the unpredictability of the Holy Spirit's leading to cultivate community than it does to make decisions through Robert's Rules of Order or some other human procedure.

The truth is, most of us leader types are not very good at maintaining our commitment to community when we gather to lead together. When caught up in the dynamics of organizational or congregational life, we naturally resort to human methods such as posturing, maneuvering, self-protective behaviors and working the system. When we experience disagreement, we are better at creating division, voting each other off the island or leaving in a huff than finding ways to come together. Sometimes we even lob lawsuits at each other, subjecting the body of Christ to a secular court system that has little understanding of the values and commitments that inform our life together in Christian community—a move expressly forbidden in the New Testament. Our vision of what we think we can achieve or what we think we need to protect takes precedence over our life together as the community of Jesus.

Spiritual community among leaders is challenging, at best, given the dynamics that come into play when people get together to lead. *Transcending our primal human instincts and false-self patterns as we lead together does not happen by accident, nor is it a capacity that is maintained and cultivated in a random or haphazard way.* Cultivating community at the leadership level requires (1) great clarity and intentional commitment to values that undergird community, (2) shared practices that help us to live our values and keep us open to the transforming presence of Christ, and (3) a clear covenant that ratifies or makes real our intent to live together this way. In most cases this process begins by asking brave questions about the organizational culture, and thoughtfully choosing practices, structures and behaviors that will help us become the community we long to be.

WHAT'S YOUR CULTURE?

Have you ever had an experience like this? You are enjoying a private conversation with another leader from within your church or organization, and the two of you are open and receptive, able to listen attentively and willing to share your thoughts from the heart. You notice a prayerful spirit in that person or perhaps a deep wisdom that you respect. Perhaps you have similar interactions with other leaders on a one-to-one basis. But when in a group setting—a board meeting, an elder meeting, a staff meeting—things are different. A person who expressed real wisdom privately is now reticent to share openheartedly. Someone who is normally kind and gentle exhibits a hard, defensive edge. Relationships that are characterized by love and trust in other settings become tense or give way to maneuvering and posturing that speak of a subtle distrust. Someone who has, in other settings, expressed the desire to know and do the will of God can barely find time for a quick prayer at the beginning of a meeting. You are confused and wonder, *What's going on here?*

This common and yet disturbing experience speaks to the power of organizational culture to shape individuals and their responses. Human beings are a lot like rocks in a riverbed. Just as the water flowing over the rocks day after day changes the shape of those rocks, we too are shaped by the flow of the organizational dynamics that are at play in the group we are a part of. These dynamics are often so subtle that it is very hard to recognize them. Sometimes there is an unspoken rule that we are not *allowed* to talk about these things. Like the townspeople in the old fable, we are afraid to state the obvious—that the emperor has no clothes! None of us wants to be the little boy who shocks everyone by acknowledging the obvious.

Brave leaders who are concerned about spiritual formation and discernment in their setting ask, How is the *organizational culture* shaping me and all others who work and worship here? Are we being transformed into people given over to the process of discerning and doing the will of God? Or are we being deformed by unhealthy organizational dynamics? Is discernment even possible in the current environment, or is there something in our group dynamics that actually prevents it?

Personal Reflection

Sit with these questions for a while. What do you notice about how the culture of your church or organization is shaping you and others? Does participation in this culture encourage and support spiritual transformation, or are there dynamics in the environment that actually work against the process of transformation?

TRANSFORMING OR DEFORMING?

Any approach to leadership discernment that fails to wrestle with the power of organizational systems will have limited spiritual effect over the long haul. One of the dangers inherent in many current approaches to spiritual formation is that it has been reduced to a private matter that can be handled through an occasional personal retreat. But spiritual transformation is not merely an individual matter.

Authentic spiritual transformation confronts us not only on the personal level, it also confronts systemic realities as well. It exposes the ways that our life together has either a transforming or a deforming effect on us, which can be a bit threatening to face. Every church or organization has its own culture—a normal way of being and working together. Margaret Wheatley describes it this way: "We can never see an organizational field; but we can see its influence by looking at behavior. To learn what's in the field, look at what people are doing. They have picked up the messages, discerned what is truly valued, and then shaped their behavior accordingly."[4]

Some of these cultural norms are addressed or made official through spoken or written communication. However, many are unspoken and involve a tacit agreement that everyone will adhere to these norms. For instance, there might be cultural patterns of addiction to work. Thus, even though staff members are entitled to a certain amount of vacation time, no one takes their full vacation or they are at least available during their vacation if needed. Or perhaps subtle norms govern what kind of information gets shared in certain settings, or how truth is manipulated to be more palatable. It could be that the senior leader has glaring character issues that are destructive to the group, but these issues are tolerated. These are but a few examples of cultural norms that may shape the organizational environment and thus the individuals who work there.

An even more subtle dynamic within churches and organizations is the spirit or the ethos of a place. Thus, in Revelation 2–3,

Christ addresses each of the seven churches as a whole rather than addressing any of the individuals who make up the whole. The spirit of a church or institution can remain fairly constant over decades, even centuries, though all the original members have long since departed. It is why a discerning person can sometimes sense a spirit of apathy and defeat in a place, or a spirit of love, trust and deep faith. The more deeply an individual engages in the life of the group, the more he or she will be shaped by the spirit of it, often without even being aware of it.

GOOD NEWS AND BAD NEWS

When it comes to transformation or deformation, organizational cultures are rarely neutral. For the most part cultural norms will support and catalyze *or* work against the process of spiritual transformation. Cultivating a culture of spiritual transformation that results in the ability to discern the will of God does not happen by accident. It *is led* very intentionally by leaders who are committed to spiritual transformation. It is led thoughtfully by leaders who are (1) clear that spiritual community is what they are called to be, (2) cultivating a culture of spiritual transformation by embracing the values that undergird community, (3) willing to engage the practices that help them live out their values in concrete ways, and (4) committed to covenant relationships. There is no shortcut for this.

The good news (and this is *very* good news!) is that a leadership group committed to spiritual transformation will automatically begin to change the culture of their community. Eventually, *living* these transforming values and behaviors together will lead to the ability to *articulate* deeply held values for the community in ways that are truly compelling. Then everyone can more intentionally commit themselves to concrete practices that will help them express those values. Over time, these values and practices become embedded in the system, which creates positive cultural norms that shape the spirit or the ethos of the place. Simply by being in the flow of the community, individuals in the community will experience life change that increases their capacity to discern and do the will of God together. These positive cultural norms begin to create a healthy system. Over time, life in community becomes a transforming experience rather than a deforming one.

In Community

PRACTICING TOGETHER

For this discussion, seek to create a safe environment in which each person's experience of the organization's or church's dynamics can be expressed and received with respect. Trust that "truth in the inward parts" and truth expressed to each other will lead to freedom and deeper levels of transformation. Know that this conversation will take time.

With honesty and mutual respect, take turns giving each person the opportunity to express what he or she has experienced and observed about participation in the life of this church or organization. Is it transforming or deforming? What is the spirit or ethos of the place? Listen to each other's experiences. Resist the urge to defend anything, to blame anyone or to "pile on." After each person has shared, there may be a longing for something different welling up within the group. Express that to each other and to God in a time of prayer, if that feels right. Confess personal and corporate sins as needed. Ask God to guide you in the process of becoming a transforming community rather than a deforming community.

CLOSING PRAYER
Forgiving God,
your Son once said
that his brother, sister, and mother
were all who did your will.

Yet even when we fail to do your will
you welcome and accept us
as your children.
Teach us to include one another
as readily as you include us;
Teach us to welcome and accept each other
as readily as you welcome and accept us;
Teach us how to be the community of Jesus,
a community that transforms rather than deforms;
for to do so is to do your heavenly will.
Amen.[5]

5

Values That
Undergird Community

The more genuine and the deeper our community becomes,
the more will everything else between us recede, the more clearly and purely
will Jesus Christ and his work become the one and only thing that is vital
between us. We have one another only through Christ, but through
Christ we do have one another, wholly, and for all eternity.

Dietrich Bonhoeffer

❧

The Grace Church leadership group was very surprised by
what happened next. With guidance from their facilitator, they
created a safe zone in which they were invited to be honest
about whether they experienced the group to be a team or a
community, and whether the way they were doing life together
in ministry was transforming or deforming. They agreed to be
respectful of each other's experiences, not to judge or dismiss
others, and to trust that whatever truth was shared would lead
to new levels of freedom, giving God good material to work
with. The elders and senior pastor assured the staff that no one
would be penalized for what was said that night and that the

perspectives shared would not be held against them. There was also a serious commitment to confidentiality.

Each person was given five to seven minutes to talk without being interrupted; they were encouraged to make "I" statements so it was clear they were speaking for themselves and from their own experience. If they wanted to, they could also say something about what they hoped life in Christian ministry could be, but it was understood that that might be more than they felt ready to share. As they listened, they were encouraged to rely on the prayer of quiet trust as a way of refraining from defending or trying to fix anything. Their only goal was to hear the person who was speaking and attempt to understand his or her experience of the group. Only clarifying questions were allowed in response.

One of the elders broke the ice by talking about how the disagreement about the property and the group splitting off had affected him. Tears welled up as he shared that he had considered the elder group to be his spiritual community, but when people he thought were friends for life had left in anger and dissension, something in him died. He admitted that he then began to relate to the whole situation in a more guarded fashion. He knew that he had been holding himself back from the group because he never wanted to go through that kind of pain again. It was lonely, but it was safer.

The next person talked about the moral failure that had taken place several years back and expressed how hard it had been to come to peace with what happened. She and her husband had been close friends with the couple whose marriage had been compromised in the affair, and yet she really didn't know how the situation had been handled behind closed doors. The couple had left abruptly with no chance to say goodbye or to talk openly and grieve the loss together. She assumed the abrupt departure was because they were ashamed and embarrassed, but it remained an open wound for her. In addition to the loss of the friendship and the shock of what happened, it felt like a taboo subject that the group couldn't talk about. Her tears flowed silently; the people on either side put their arms around her and let her cry.

After she recovered, the next person—one of the worship pastors—picked up on that situation and mentioned that it had also seemed to introduce such fear among the men and women in the group that they had become very guarded around each other. Although he wanted to speak in generalities, he disciplined himself to make an "I" statement: "I know that I have withdrawn from the women in the group because I just don't know how to relate to them anymore, and I'm so sorry for that. But I just keep thinking, *If it could happen to Paul it could happen to me.* What does it even mean to be in community with people of the opposite gender?" In addition, some questioned whether the elders had been too harsh in their handling of the matter. For those in touch with their own vulnerability, the idea that the elders could be that harsh was frightening, which raised another obstacle between them.

The person who spoke next was the assistant to several of the pastors. She shared that because she was "just an administrative person" she consistently felt like she was on the outside of most decision-making processes—even those decisions that affected her. Even though she had the gift of discernment, she felt that because she was support staff rather than pastoral staff, that gift would never be fully received. In fact, she wasn't sure how to offer it. She wasn't sure she was even a part of the community in the same way everyone else was.

Perhaps the most revealing comment came from the executive pastor. He had come on board a couple years earlier—transitioning from a successful career in business to tackle the operational aspects of the church. He had been excited to bring what he had always thought of as "secular" gifts to a spiritual endeavor, and he had assumed that this experience would help integrate the different parts of himself into a more seamless whole. He had looked forward to a quality of working relationships that would be different from what he had experienced in the marketplace. His voice broke a little as he admitted that he had experienced more community in the secular marketplace than he did at the church. His comments were not made with any sort of blame or belligerence, which made them all the more powerful. He said that at least in the business world he knew where he stood, but in a church environment, where people spiritualized things so much, he couldn't always tell what was going on. When he joined the staff, he thought he was joining a community in which he would grow and change for the better; instead, he noticed that he was getting more cynical and hardened in his approach to church and even in his own spiritual life.

Finally, the small groups pastor, who had been with the church from the early days, talked about how the pace of life had intensified over the years and how hard it was to keep up. As they kept adding church services and outreach ministries that required evening commitments, it had put a real strain on his marriage and family, but he didn't know what to do. Ministry was his whole life, and besides that, he needed the job. He had gotten wind of the fact that the elders were evaluating whether they had "the right people on the bus," and he was afraid he was on the bubble. How in the world was he supposed to feel like this was a safe community for him? What started out as the shared passion of a few like-minded souls had become a performance treadmill that kept him running faster and faster, trying to keep up with a set of expectations that seemed beyond his capacity. He trembled as he spoke; he couldn't believe that he was saying these things in front of the elders who could fire him. But he was desperate for change and to find a better way to live. Tonight he was willing to take the risk and trust that the process they were being guided in would take them to good places in the end.

There was more—much more—but you get the idea. When everyone had finished sharing, the group sat together in reverent, stunned silence. No one tried to fix anything or tie it up with a pretty bow. They just sat there, not really believing what they had done. So many tears had been shed, so much truth had been spoken. Had they really said all those things after holding it in for so long? Had they dared to be that open in a work environment? Was it really going to be okay? Since they had been learning to recognize consolation and desolation, they weren't thrown by the surface emotion of fear and uncertainty; the deeper reality was the sense of peace that flowed underneath it all and the recognition that this indeed was the quality of life and relationship they had been longing for. Tonight they had visited the reality called spiritual community; now they wanted to learn how to live there. More words seemed completely irrelevant so they said night prayers and went to bed.

A HOLY ENDEAVOR

Once a leadership group has developed this longing for community and experienced the "conversion to community"—in other words, they are committed to becoming a transforming community—the first step is to articulate the values and principles that will guide them in this holy endeavor. Once shared values have been articulated, the group can identify those practices that will help them live their values in concrete ways; then they can establish a covenant with each other, which "ratifies" or makes their commitment real. But they have to start with articulating their values.

Values are not ideals; they are actual ways of being and qualities of character that are real and possible for human beings, although living them often comes at a price. One way we know values are real is that we have already experienced them somewhere on some level. Otherwise, we would neither know they existed nor try to articulate them. When we talk about deeply held values, we are not articulating something that is pulled out of thin air or achieved through some sort of an intellectual exercise. Rather, we are naming something that already exists—something that we have known and have experienced positively *or* that has been violated with such a devastating effect that we know in our bones how much it really matters. The Spirit witnesses with our spirit about things that are true and essential for human life and well-being; from that place of deep knowing we are willing to name them and to cry out in hope that God would enable us to live them.

The values that matter most come from deep inside the individuals involved, from the aspirations that have called the group together and from the commitments that have shaped their existence. Gordon Cosby writes about his experience founding Church of the Savior in Washington, D.C.

> Our written commitment has grown out of our life together. The life occurred first and then it was put down in a written commitment. To make a formal commitment without having drunk deeply of the life of the group is simply to take a husk that can mock us. Only in commitment can there be real belonging.[1]

FROM THE INSIDE OUT

Some values are very general and foundational; other values are more specific to the unique calling of each community and the particularities of their shared life. Whether general or particular, each leadership group will need to identify and articulate their values in ways that are biblically sound, relationally healthy, spiritually enlivening and *meaningfully expressed* in their context.

The process of establishing values and principles begins with asking members of the group to get in touch with their own personal stories, both positive and negative. Individuals are encouraged to become very clear about what values *they need to know are in place* in order for them to lean into the group as a trustworthy community. They are given the opportunity to share these values with the group and even rank them, differentiating between values that are absolutely essential for their full participation in the group life (nonnegotiables) and those that are nice, but not essential.

This part of the process assumes that individuals have a certain level of self-awareness—that is, they are in touch with their own story, have processed it enough to understand what it means and what is important to them, and are able to offer this wisdom and sense of self to the group. This wisdom is not abrasive or imposing, but is the product of "an individual effort to accurately experience and understand the world, make judgments, and decide responsible courses of action."[2]

A responsible course of action for all of us is knowing what is nonnegotiable for us in terms of the values we live by, both individually and corporately. Of course, no group will live perfectly according to their agreed-upon values, but it can be a grave mistake to place ourselves in groups that do not have a clearly articulated set of values that they seek to live with integrity.

OUR STORY AND GOD'S STORY

Another important step in the process of establishing guiding values and principles is to get in touch with the story of the group we belong to so we can identify what matters to the group. The group's story includes (1) what initially drew us together (what we valued), (2) what we have learned to value along the way (often through the school of hard knocks!), (3) how our values have shaped us in positive ways and (4) how we have been broken when we have failed to live our values consistently. This part of the conversation has the potential to take us to some of the most tender experiences of our shared life, revisiting the passion and high hopes we began with, amazing moments when God gave us the ability to live our values well (maybe even under duress) and painful moments when we fell short of living our deepest values.

In the context of such honest reflections we might discover how far we have drifted from the values that sparked our community into being; thus, part of the process of establishing or clarifying values might be to remember the charisms (gifts/graces) and the passion of the founders. This should be done periodically because we are so easily distracted by external pressures that we lose touch with who we fundamentally *are*. The irony, of course, is that we may find ourselves fighting to "stay alive" in the external world while our fundamental reason for existing has slowly evaporated.

In her book *Finding Our Way Home*, Killian Noe writes:

> Organizations and communities can lose touch with their core, their essence, their soul. The two things which put them at risk of losing their soul are time and growth. . . . Over time they tend to drift from the core truths and convictions upon which they were founded and as they grow bigger, keeping those core convictions central grows more and more difficult. . . . The core or soul of an organization is too deep to be described directly. Therefore, stories must be used to talk "around" that which is so true and so deep it defies definition. When the Israelites were forced to live as exiles in Babylon they wondered, "How do we sing the Lord's song— how do we stay connected to that which is most true about us—in a strange land?" They held onto their essence through telling and remembering their stories.[3]

The process of establishing core values and principles that will shape our life together must include allowing individuals to talk about the values important to them and also to let the group tell stories about important corporate values and how they became important. John English calls this activity "sharing our personal and communal graced history," through which we mine the gold that is present in these stories and claim that which is of greatest value. This tender but true "re-membering" takes us a long way toward knowing and naming the values that have guided our life together and will have important implications for how we will go on from here. Taking time to remember in this fashion has the possibility to powerfully integrate what was given in the past with what is being given in the present and what we are seeking in the future.

FINDING OURSELVES IN THE BIBLICAL STORY

Another important aspect of establishing guiding values and principles can be "finding ourselves" in the biblical story and allowing the values embodied in that story to shape our story. Sometimes, at the beginning of an organization's life, there is a Scripture that sparks or informs those beginnings. Of course, there will be lots of Scriptures that apply over the years, but there also will be some special Scripture that touched the organization's deep longings and was instrumental in calling it forth.

I'm not sure the Transforming Center would still be in existence if it weren't for the fact that we found ourselves so clearly in the biblical story. We were birthed from longing—the longing a few leaders had to be together in ways that were truly transforming—and from the way that certain Scriptures touched that longing with hope they could be fulfilled.

When we began this venture, we were all leaders in a variety of ministry settings where we were achieving some level of effectiveness and success. But we were missing something. We were missing a place where we could be with other leaders—not just to work together, socialize and network, or even to be inspired to be better leaders—but to attend to our ongoing process of spiritual transformation in relative anonymity.

We were tired of always being "on" and being told how to work harder and better. We were sure there had to be more to the spiritual life in leadership than hard work and hiding our true selves and our true desires. We were willing to make a significant investment of time, energy and even financial resources in order to seek "more." We wanted transformation—real change in the deep places of our hearts and lives—and we couldn't help but believe that whatever changes happened in our leadership as a result of this transformation would be for the better.

Our identity was profoundly shaped by finding ourselves in a particular place in the biblical story and allowing our values and calling to emerge from that place. We were drawn to the very beginnings of Jesus' public ministry when he made the radical choice to carry out his ministry in and through an intimate community rather than choosing to do it alone. Even though there was much in Scripture for us to reflect on regarding Jesus' relationship with his disciples, we were particularly compelled by two phrases in Mark 3. The first was in verse 13 which says that he called to himself "those whom he wanted." "Huh!" we thought. "Are we really allowed to do that—to call people together because they are the ones we want to be with?" For some reason, that was an entirely new and refreshing thought! I guess we thought it was more spiritual to do ministry with people who drove us nuts!

Then we noticed in verse 14 that Jesus first invited them "to be with him." Then he sent them out to proclaim the message and minister to others with spiritual authority. "He went up to the mountain and called to him those whom he wanted, and they came to him. And he appointed twelve, whom he also named apostles, to be with him, and to be sent out to proclaim the message" (Mk 3:13-14). Since we were all part of groups that gathered primarily around a mission where everyone's value to the group was their ability to contribute to the mission, this too was a refreshing ideal. The idea that we could gather first of all *to be together* around the presence of Christ in life-transforming ways was a truly winsome thought. We sensed that eventually a mission would emerge from our togetherness (given the fact that most of us were leader types), but that was not why we first assembled. We first gathered on the basis of our shared desire to be together with Christ and with each other in life-transforming ways.

Over time we did begin to sense God's calling to *do* something together, so we crafted a mission statement, developed ministry offerings and put structures in place to enable us to carry out our mission. All fledgling ministries do this hard work. But it was important that we first knew *who we were*. To clarify our mission and calling before we had a clear identity as a group would have

put the cart way before the horse. So based on what we could observe about Christ's relationships with his chosen ones and our
own desire to experience deeper levels of spiritual transformation
in the context of community, we committed ourselves to be together in life-transforming ways.

As we studied and reflected on the dynamics of spiritual transformation, we also discovered that spiritual transformation is not
an end in itself—it *leads to* the ability to discern and do the will of
God. With that last piece of the puzzle in place, we were able to
identify ourselves as "a community of men and women gathered
around the presence of Christ for the purpose of spiritual transformation so that we can discern and do the will of God." This
identity and the values associated with it have held through the
years, in part because our longings led us to find ourselves and
ground ourselves in a particular place in the biblical story. This in
turn motivated us to clarify and articulate values that would shape
us into the kind of community we longed to become.

VALUES THAT EMERGE FROM THE STORY

Elizabeth O'Connor of Church of the Savior writes, "While there is
something to be gained in the more conceptual and abstract
statement, something is lost when we do not tell the story of how it
was for us, and with us, when we took seriously the truths about
which we preach and write."[4] I think this is true, so I am going to
try and tell "the story of how it was for us"—how some of our values
came to be lived and eventually articulated—as an example of one
group's process of establishing guiding values and principles.

Five of our values—community, transformation, discernment,
equality and inclusiveness, lived experience—called us into being.
Other values emerged later or were articulated even more clearly
on the basis of our education in the school of hard knocks.

Community. From the very beginning we identified ourselves as
a community who gathers around the presence of Christ. We have

sought to pattern our relationships after Christ's relationships with his disciples: "He loved his own until the end" (Jn 13:1; 15; 17). Thus, coming together and staying together in unity is our first and most enduring task—no matter how imperfectly we do it. *What we do* flows out of *who we are* in Christ.

Our commitment to being a community has been and continues to be the most essential thing about us. We knew that if we called ourselves a leadership team, a management team, a board or a cabinet, that might be all we would get—a method of governing that is basically secular in its orientation, with a few spiritual elements thrown in. At the very least we would have to work hard not to let that terminology define us according to whatever expectations normally go along with it. Language really does shape reality.

When we understand ourselves to be—and actually call ourselves—a leadership *community*, we are shaped by and called to a different set of expectations, which are spiritual in nature. This language reminds us of who we are called to be and what we have committed ourselves to. What we call things really matters.

Seeking to follow Christ together and carrying out the mission he has given us *as a spiritual community* is a lot more demanding than being a team or an organization. We have not done it perfectly, and there have certainly been times when the demands of being a community rather than an organization have seemed like too much! Sometimes people want to join us precisely because we are seeking to live out community values in the context of ministry, but then they are surprised when our commitments demand more of them than what they expected. This is never easy. But we have learned compromising community means compromising our essence. If this happens, we would not have much of value to offer to others. A significant part of our ongoing transformation involves wrestling with what it means to be a community gathered around the presence of Christ even though we are a not-for-profit entity with all that that requires.

The value of community is the most challenging and demanding value we are committed to together, but it is actually the value we find most compelling.

Spiritual transformation. We are also convinced that the best thing any of us brings to leadership is our own transforming self. In fact, the ability to come together and stay together in unity is *a direct result* of a continuing process of spiritual transformation as individuals and also in our life together. Our commitment to spiritual transformation means that each person in leadership is committed to a personal rule of life—spiritual rhythms that keep us open to and available for God's transforming work so that we are bringing a transforming self to leadership as an act of worship (Rom 12:1).

It is not enough for individual leaders to be committed to their own personal transformation; we are also committed to being a *transforming* community—making sure that our life together has a transforming effect on the individuals involved. This means we have a rule of life for our community as well. We are always asking, Is the culture of our life in community transforming or deforming? It's a tough question and it is always a question that needs to be asked.

Leadership discernment. We are committed to the *habit* of discernment—seeking to be attentive and alert to God's activity in and among us so that we can respond faithfully. We are also committed to the *practice* of discernment in community—proactively seeking God's guidance together when we need specific direction for decision making. Because discernment takes more time and a different kind of attention than decision making, this requires commitment to a clear process for leadership discernment (which I will describe more fully in chaps. 10-12) and the discipline to carry it out.

Most of us in leadership in the Transforming Center have a natural bent toward strategic thinking and planning. But every time we have made decisions purely from the standpoint of what is strategic rather than entering first into a process of discernment, we have gotten ahead of ourselves and made mistakes. Just because something is strategic does not necessarily mean it is God's will for us right now.

When we take time and make space to listen to what God is saying to us in the deeper places of our being, we usually find that less is more. We have been humbled by this on more than one occasion. This is a defining characteristic of any truly spiritual community—the shared commitment to move forward as we are led by the Spirit, not by our own thinking and planning. We are not opposed to planning; in fact, it is an important second step. But we are committed to discernment—listening deeply for God's direction—as the precursor to any plans we make. And we are committed to continue listening as we move forward with those plans. When we feel we have, to the best of our ability, discerned God's will, we can then move confidently and with measured pace into the planning stages.

Equality and inclusiveness. Equality and inclusiveness have been a part of our identity from the very beginning because the particular people God called together believe and affirm that in Christ "there is no longer Jew or Greek, there is no longer slave or free, there is no longer male and female; for all of you are one in Christ Jesus" (Gal 3:28). Each of us, in our own way, had arrived at the theological and biblical conclusion that individuals find their place and bring their gifts to Christian community on the basis of their relationship *with* God, their calling *from* God and their gifting *by* God (1 Cor 12). Human beings are not to be defined or limited on the basis of outward characteristics such as race, socioeconomic status or gender—in the church or anywhere else! God has graced us with unity on this issue.

The primary metaphor Scripture utilizes to describe our relationships in the body of Christ is that of a family—brothers and sisters growing in love and learning to serve in harmony—which we take literally and seriously. In a healthy family, brothers and sisters are equally loved, valued and given opportunities to develop their talents and spiritual gifts. As women and men in community we work together with Christ and each other on the basis of spiritual gifts and calling. We seek to include one another—across lines of race, gender and socioeconomic status—in all aspects of life and ministry. We respect what each person contributes to the life of the community.[5]

Lived experience. Early on we agreed that we would not teach theories or concepts we merely wished were true. In fact, we actually wanted to *experience* transformation in community even more than we wanted to teach it! When it came time for us to teach, we agreed to follow Jesus' example in his conversation with Nicodemus: "We speak of what we know and testify to what we have seen" (Jn 3:5). Sometimes we choose not to teach on certain topics— even great topics!—because we know we are not yet living them effectively. This does not mean we have to have lived things perfectly in order to teach them; it does mean, however, that we only teach those things we value and are trying to live *with integrity*, communicating honestly about our successes and our failures.

Self-knowledge and personal responsibility. Closely related to our commitment to spiritual transformation is our commitment to increasing levels of self-knowledge and our willingness to take responsibility for negative patterns that affect our interactions in community. We are intentional about dealing with our own inner dynamics appropriately as we become aware of them.

Spiritual transformation takes place primarily in those places where we are not like Christ. In community, others become agents of God's troubling grace, giving us many opportunities to see ourselves more clearly, to repent and to confess our sins one to another in order to receive grace and healing.[6] Thus, we seek to respect the profound role that acknowledging our brokenness plays in the unfolding of the spiritual life and in the formation of true spiritual community. We believe that coming face to face with our weakness and being honest about it opens us to the gift of community and also releases God's power among us, within us, beyond us (2 Cor 12:7-10). Confessing our brokenness fosters humility as we serve together.

Without the willingness to name sin, to cultivate self-awareness relative to what causes our negative behavior and to confess our sins one to another as needed, communities tend to splinter and fall apart under pressure—an inevitability that undermines Jesus' deepest desire for our oneness as expressed in John 17. Growing self-knowledge is a crucial aspect of engaging fruitfully in a discernment process because it reduces the risk of the community falling apart due to people not being willing or able to own their negative patterns and sins.

Truth. The psalmist says, "You desire truth in the inward being; therefore teach me wisdom in my secret heart" (Ps 51:6). There are many reasons why the ability to know the truth, tell the truth and live in the truth is so important for community life. One reason is that truth leads to freedom, spiritual transformation and deeper levels of discernment. All truth, no matter how delicate, painful or seemingly inconsequential, can contribute to the process of transformation and to the ability to discern faithfully. Since the Holy Spirit is given to us to guide us into truth, rather than hiding or "spinning" the truth, we seek to offer the truth to one another in love and gentleness. Anything less than clear, honest communication patterns places the community in great peril. The story of Ananias and Sapphira illustrates the point.

This story took place very early in the history of the New Testament church, when the new community of Jesus was being established through the work of the Holy Spirit. One evidence of the Spirit's work was that the disciples and new converts were "of one heart and soul, and no one claimed private ownership of any possessions, but everything they owned was held in common." People were selling their possessions and sharing with anyone in need. Because of the Spirit's grace, "there was not a needy person among them" (Acts 4:32-33).

In the midst of this outpouring of grace, Ananias and Sapphira

sold a piece of property and led the disciples to believe they were offering all the money they had received from the sale. When Peter ex-
posed this, they were struck dead immediately. Why? It was *not* because they had kept some of the proceeds for themselves. Peter was
careful to point out that they were free to do whatever they wished
with their property. But they had lied to the community of faith, and
in so doing had lied to God. "How is it that you have contrived this
deed in your heart? You did not lie to us but to God" (Acts 5:4).

Why was this lack of honesty so serious in God's eyes? Because
*when we fail to be truthful with each other, we strike at the heart of
community and undermine its viability.* Only as we speak the truth
in love do we *grow up* in Christ and become the mature body of
Christ (Eph 4:15). It is impossible to be in community without a
commitment to truth telling. Other kinds of groups might be able
to function on some level without truth telling, but there will not
be the spiritual community we are describing here.

Because knowing the truth and living in truth is such a deeply
held value, it guides us and gives us courage to say the hard thing
with grace and love, and to support each other in doing so.

Lovingkindness. Of course, the commitment to truth telling
must also be balanced with love and kindness. Kindness is a basic
characteristic of mature spirituality, but the Christian community
is often unkind. Those who gathered to form the Transforming
Center had been around the Christian leadership block enough
times to experience this fact for ourselves. As we clarified our
values, we mused, "Wouldn't it be something if, at the very least,
we could form a place where we (and those we minster to) experienced true kindness and gentleness over the long haul?" If that's
all we accomplished, it would be significant to the kingdom! As
we talked, it became clear that we wanted to add lovingkindness
to the list of values we would flesh out together.

Gratitude. We stumbled into gratitude almost by accident, but
over time it has developed into a full-blown commitment. Here's

how it happened: On the second night of our very first retreat together, we decided to get a little bit more dressed up and enjoy each other's company over a special dinner to celebrate how God had met us throughout our time together. The first day had been typical— praying the hours, being challenged by good teaching, seeking God in solitude and sharing with each other around matters of the soul. On the second night it just felt good (and God-honoring) to celebrate in God's presence with good fun, good food and good conversation. Our dinnertime conversation quite naturally revolved around noticing specific instances of God's goodness, guidance and grace, which turned into a celebration of all we were grateful for.

That time of celebration was so energizing and important that it became our pattern. Over time we experienced celebration as the spiritual discipline associated with gratitude. We began looking for opportunities to celebrate God's presence and activity among us. To this day our retreats always have one evening that is specifically designed for celebration. We now start leadership meetings with a time of recounting where we have seen God at work so we can celebrate together. For us, gratitude is more than just a warm, fuzzy experience; it is a powerful practice that is good for the soul. In Romans 1:21 Paul writes of those who by their wickedness suppress the truth: "for though they knew God, they did not honor him as God or give thanks to him, but they became futile in their thinking, and their senseless minds were darkened." Any practice that can stave off futile thinking and dark minds is worth investing in!

Conflict transformation. One of the most important aspects of long-term community is agreeing to very concrete commitments regarding how we will handle the inevitable conflict. All relationships go through a honeymoon stage when it seems like nothing can go wrong and relational conflicts could never happen to us. Don't be fooled by the euphoria of those early days. Conflict happens in all relationships; the only question is what we will do when it does. So before this happens, we need to ask whether we are com-

mitted enough to stay together and discern what God is doing in
and among us when conflict or differing perspectives arise.

We went through several difficult experiences before we realized that we needed to define and clarify the value of conflict
transformation. This is not a commitment to transforming the
conflict (as valuable as that is); rather, it is a commitment for *us to
seek transformation in and through the conflict*. We noted that Jesus'
promise "Where two or three are gathered in my name, I am there
among them" was not about people gathered for worship or prayer
but to those gathered specifically to deal with conflict! To those
who are brave enough to engage conflict openly in Christ's
presence, a special promise of Christ's presence is given. So in the
midst of conflict we are committed to seek transformation by

1. finding ways to be open to the transforming presence of Christ,
   even in the midst of conflict and disagreement (Mt 18:17),
   through prayer, solitude and silence, self-examination, and
   spiritual direction

2. honoring God and expressing our love for Jesus by valuing
   what he values—love and unity (Jn 17)

3. pursuing deeper levels of transformation in and through conflict rather than capitulating to what is worst within us by
   asking God, What part of this conflict is about me?

Commitment to engaging conflict in a way that changes us *for
the better* and deepens our unity in Christ is more challenging than
conflict management or conflict resolution, and it is certainly the
opposite of conflict avoidance. It is important to agree together on
what constitutes a biblical and spiritual process, and then commit
to adhere to it. We also need to empower the group to call each
other back to these commitments during difficult times.

This value was clarified much later in our community's development, but it is now one of our defining values. We talk about it

in detail with anyone who joins us at the board level, as an employee or volunteer, and in significant contractual relationships or partnerships. We know that our good work on all the other values can be nullified in one heart-stopping moment if people refuse to work through conflict in life-transforming ways, and we are no longer willing to risk it.

Confidentiality and conflict of interest. Because we work together with such openness, we exercise great care *not* to do anything that might be a conflict of interest or not in the best interest of the Transforming Center community and ministries. We also adhere to a strict confidentiality agreement regarding personal information about anyone involved with us and also regarding leadership matters and decisions. Our intent is to clarify and foster in each of us a *spirit* of *choosing* to make decisions that are good for the Transforming Center community and those who are giving sacrificially to it. These are values that we could easily assume all Christians embrace, but it's not necessarily so.

Personal Reflection

As a leader in your current community context, what values and principles are necessary for you to engage fully and freely? Be ready to share these with the leadership group you are a part of.

WHEN ALL ELSE FAILS

Years ago I had the opportunity to have a face-to-face conversation with Gordon Cosby, founding pastor of Church of the Savior in Washington, D.C. I have such great respect for Gordon—what he's done and how he's done it for over fifty years—that I wanted to be prepared with my most burning question: *Is there ever any reason to violate the value of community?*

I had been in settings where the values undergirding community were violated in such profound ways that I wondered if this was inevitable in ministry. I hoped this wasn't the case, but since I tend to be too idealistic and need others to help me be realistic, Gordon would be my reality check. If he said there are times when community values could be violated, I was at least willing to consider it.

So I asked my question and could hardly breathe as I waited for his answer. Without hesitation he said, "No, there is never a reason to violate community, because then you have violated your essence and you have nothing of value to offer to anyone." I was relieved; in the depths of my being, I knew this was right.

But I also knew that we do violate community—not because we intend to but because we are human. What happens then? In times of pain and disillusionment it is tempting to say, "Well, that didn't work! I'm never going to try *that* again." But where does that leave us? With no vision. With merely a life of survival and self-protection, which is not reason enough to live.

So here is my conclusion: When all else has failed and we have failed each other, there is still the Story—the story of Jesus, who lived according to a powerful set of values that must have seemed just as impossible then as they do now. It is a story that inspires us every time. With each loss and each gain, each setback and each step forward, there is always this sense of "Where else would we go? What else would we want to shoot for?" And so we find ourselves in the Story again. We get in touch with what we value most deeply. As God works in us, we repent of our failure to fully embrace our values. And we try again—only this time with more wisdom.

In Community

PRACTICING TOGETHER

Take time to identify and describe the following:

1. Guiding values and principles that shape your identity as a

community in positive ways. What are they? How have they shaped you for good?

2. Values that have shaped your life in community in the past but from which you have drifted. What caused these to slip? Would you like to reclaim them? What would that look like?

3. Values and principles that you now know are necessary to shape your life together as a transforming community. (Some will be general and appropriate to any Christian community; others might be unique to your particular situation and cultural milieu.)

Name these values and guiding principles (maybe at a longer retreat or during several sessions that are part of your normal meeting rhythm). Affirm their importance and record them in words that are compelling to each of you in your unique context.

End your time with the following closing prayer. Choose one person to read the nonitalic parts and then have the rest of the group read the italic parts as a response.

CLOSING PRAYER

O God, you have taught us to keep all your commandments by loving you and our neighbor.

Grant us the grace of your Holy Spirit,
that we may be devoted to you with our whole heart,
and united to one another with pure affection;

through Jesus Christ our Lord,
who lives and reigns with you and the Holy Spirit,
one God, forever and ever.

All: *Amen.*[7]

6

PRACTICES FOR OPENING
TO GOD TOGETHER

*No one grows by doing what someone else forces us to do. We begin
to grow when we finally want to grow. All the rigid fathers and
demanding mothers and disapproving teachers in the world
cannot make up for our own decision to become
what we can by doing what we must.*

JOAN CHITTISTER

&

The Grace Church leadership group awoke the morning after their sharing having rested well and feeling ready to continue their conversation about becoming a community for discernment. They spent the morning talking about guiding values and principles. These included the values of the church at its foundation and those needed to create a safe community now. The group was grateful for the presence of an outside facilitator because everyone was able to participate fully and on a level playing field.

Community was the first value they agreed on together. The experience of community they tasted the previous evening (and in the months leading up to it) confirmed that they wanted to experience the reality of spiritual community at the leadership level. Their commitment to personal transformation and spiritual friendships made it possible for them to share at a deeper level, so they made the commitment to become a *transforming community*. Next they committed to *telling the truth and fostering honest, open communication.* Their earlier experience of sharing so openly had caused them to realize how far they had gotten from the honesty and transparency that had characterized the group in their early days. They also realized how destructive it was to the community's life when they weren't able to be honest about important matters that affected them all. They longed for healthier and more God-honoring patterns in their communication.

The group also discussed conflict transformation. They had never considered that there might be more to dealing with conflict than managing or resolving it. They realized that they did not know how to deal with conflict in a transforming way. Being open to the presence of Christ in conflictual situations was a completely new and refreshing idea for them. They realized no matter what else they were doing well, if they didn't have some way to approach conflict, it could negate everything else. Even though they didn't know exactly how to practice conflict transformation, they wanted to affirm it as a value and then explore concrete ways to practice it. They asked their facilitator if she could help them with this, which she agreed to do.

The conversation that morning was energizing and hopeful. They felt like a different group than they had been just a few months earlier. By the end of the morning they had five or six values clearly articulated. They agreed that they were free to add more as others became clear. Rather than list so many that it felt overwhelming, they wanted to focus on a few they could embrace fully before they added any more.

In the late afternoon session their facilitator began with a story illustrating the need for the next step—identifying concrete practices that would help them live their values. She told them about helping the staff and elders of a large church consider their commitment to spiritual transformation and then eventually guiding them in a process of discernment.

"They did some really good work," she said. "They established guiding values and principles. They captured those values and principles in writing and designed a very sharp document that was distributed to everyone concerned. They learned about leadership discernment and agreed they wanted to try it. We worked through a discernment process regarding an important issue on which they were quite polarized, and the Spirit worked through the process to bring them to a unanimous decision. They were ecstatic! The congregation was ecstatic! They were sold on the process and committed themselves as leaders to continue growing as a community that would use discernment for future decision making.

"I didn't hear from them for several months.

"The next time someone from the church made contact with me it was the staff member with whom I had worked most closely in setting up my visits with them. He let me know that since we had been together last, the elders had fired the senior pastor, the small groups pastor, the spiritual formation pastor and maybe others—I can't remember now. It was a major shakedown that came as a complete shock to those involved. After all the work they had done together to cultivate spiritual community, to establish guiding values and principles, and to commit themselves to leadership discernment as a way of making decisions, apparently that commitment didn't hold in the face of whatever issues they were facing.

"Even though they had articulated their commitment to be a community of discernment, for whatever reason they did not discern this one together. The disillusionment on the part of the staff who thought they were part of a *leadership community* was deep and wide."

Needless to say, the Grace Church leaders were sobered by this story and they were ready to hear about practices that would prevent that kind of thing from happening to them!

THE COMMUNITY SQUEEZE

Articulating values—and even having a graphic designer develop a compelling document that captures them—does not guarantee that a group will be able to live by them. All of us struggle with staying true to our values in the rough and tumble of leadership. When decisions need to be made and action needs to be taken, it is hard to trust that the Spirit's presence and activity can bring about unity. So we capitulate to posturing and maneuvering, secret meetings, heavy-handed tactics and top-down pronouncements. It isn't God we trust in such moments. When push comes to shove, we trust in familiar methods that make us feel safe and in control. There is not a lot of space for God to work in these methods, and I suspect that, at times, that is exactly what we want.

Another reason it is hard to live by our values in the rough and tumble of leadership is that somehow the mission always wants to overtake our essence as a community gathered around the presence of Christ. No matter how committed we are to community there is always the temptation to allow the demands of ministry to squeeze out the time it takes to cultivate community. As much as we are committed to discernment, sometimes decisions get made too quickly, without enough time to listen fully to the wisdom of the whole community.

Speaking personally again about our experience in the Transforming Center, even though our group coalesced around a shared desire to discern and do the will of God both personally and in community, we have been stunned when individuals have made significant decisions without engaging a process of community discernment. Even though we are committed to spiritual rhythms, at times we have been too ambitious with our planning and then struggled to keep up with the pace of life that our plans required. Even though celebration is one of our favorite disciplines, we have missed opportunities to celebrate what God is doing among us because we thought we didn't have time. And at times we have gotten so caught up with what we are offering to others that our personal and shared disciplines have suffered. How does this happen? What dynamics are at work here?

First, it is very hard to resist the temptation to value *doing* over *being* and *becoming*. This is a function of our human nature, which has been exacerbated by current trends within the Christian community that seem to value successes that can be seen and measured. This is one difference between our assumed spirituality (what we would like to believe about ourselves) and our actual or functional spirituality (what is true about our practice). We want to believe that we hold a certain set of values, and we would like others to believe that we hold them as well, but when the rubber meets the road of life in leadership, it is much harder to live our values than we imagined. It is all too easy to capitulate to that which is most deeply ingrained within us.

Commitment to community—especially at the leadership level—is profoundly countercultural. It goes against the grain of the West's Lone Ranger mindset, which elevates independence to a virtue. It also flies in the face of our consumer mindset that sees everything as a commodity to be used and then discarded. Often, we are not even aware that we have compromised our values until it's too late. Clearly, the dynamics that drive this behavior are more powerful than our good intentions. This is why we need practices—concrete activities, experiences, attitudes and relating patterns—that will help us be who we say we are and live our intentions together.

Once individuals in a group are on a transforming path individually, after they have experienced the conversion to community and have established guiding values, then we need to ask:

- What are the practices, relationships and experiences that will help us stay in a process of spiritual transformation—together?

- What practices will help us stay open to the presence of Christ in our midst so that we can discern God's will together?

- How can we order our life together so we are becoming increasingly abandoned to God rather than being driven by our egos and caught up in our own compulsions?

In order to answer these questions we can turn to the ancient practice of creating a rule of life. This is simply a regular pattern of attitudes, behaviors and practices that—as we submit to them over time—create space and opportunity for Christ to be more fully formed in us. Spiritual leaders like Augustine, Benedict, Francis of Assisi and Teresa of Ávila developed a set of practices or rhythms designed to govern the shared life of the monks and nuns living in community. These practices had the same purpose then that they do now—to provide ways of surrendering our negative patterns and sinful behaviors so that we can be shaped by new ones as we do life together. They also help us open ourselves more intentionally to the presence and activity of God in our lives.

Since a spiritual community exists to be responsive to the transforming presence of Christ so that we can discern and do the will of God, our practices must be consistent with this overarching purpose. Life in community can never be about merely getting a job done—as important as that is. It must also always take into account *how* we get the job done and whether we are transformed or deformed in the process. A community's spiritual rhythms (or rule of life) will be unique—based on the particularities of its situation—and the *spirit* in which the members undertake these practices is of utmost importance. Brian Taylor puts it this way:

> To live according to a tradition and under a rule of life, whether Benedict's or someone else's, is to enter consciously into a process of growth in grace and to undertake a specific

discipline used in that process. However, a rule of life is not undertaken for its own sake so that one can "become disciplined," as if that were a primary virtue. The need for order can be an extremely neurotic form of self-control when it is no longer a means to reach God but, rather, an end in itself. The discipline of a rule of life is undertaken as a means to freedom in God.[1]

Although it may seem contradictory, committing to a rule of life together is actually a means of great freedom, as Taylor points out. It is the freedom of having our life together oriented toward one goal—opening to the transforming work of Christ so that we can discern and do his will. When we open to God together through a common rule of life, even a moment of silence can be very powerful. Conversely, when practices are viewed as obligatory duties—something to get out of the way so we can get to the "real business" of the meeting—even the most well thought out devotional will have little impact. Following are several practices that we have embraced to shape our own rule of life in community.

PRACTICING TRANSFORMATION
Our first shared commitment is that each of us has established a personal rule of life. Including personal rhythms as one aspect of our community commitment acknowledges the fact that the process of spiritual transformation is not for self alone; it is for the glory of God, the abundance of our own lives and *for the sake of others*. Individuals not engaged in regular spiritual practices will engage the leadership setting as an untransformed self, stuck in all the particularities of their false-self patterns.

On the other hand, those engaged regularly in spiritual practices can't help but bring a transforming presence into the leadership setting. They are not fully transformed and definitely not perfect, but always "on the way" and engaging the group with a view to transformation. For us, that means that each leader goes through our two-year Transforming Community® experience, a foundational corporate discipline in which we learn and practice key spiritual disciplines—fixed-hour prayer; solitude, silence and retreat; sane rhythms of work and rest (including sabbath); reading and reflecting on Scripture; honoring the body as a spiritual discipline; self-examination and confession; personal and leadership discernment; spiritual direction; and celebration.[2]

This two-year immersion experience culminates with each individual crafting a personal rule of life. Thus we know each person in leadership has a plan for an ongoing process of transformation—not just in theory but in well-informed practice. This has become our board orientation process; once we have shared these life-shaping practices together in the Transforming Community experience, we naturally carry them over into our leadership. By the time we enter into leadership together, we each have a personal rule of life and freely check in with each other about how we are maintaining our rhythms. We talk about our pace of life and whether it is promoting health or is leading to exhaustion. When scheduling, we look not only at the strategic opportunities but also whether these opportunities will enable us to maintain a life-giving way of life. Commitment to a rule of life is so significant to our corporate well-being that completion of the Transforming Community experience is a prerequisite for being a leader in the Transforming Center. The best thing a person can bring to leadership is his or her own transforming self.

While you might not have the ability to put such an elaborate process in place, your leaders could participate in a Transforming Community experience or a similar spiritual formation program. Or you could have leaders read and work through *Sacred Rhythms*, which culminates in the process of developing a rule of life. Doing this with a spiritual friend or a spiritual director would be even better. You might consider having ongoing sacred rhythms classes so the whole congregation or organization is participating in the process—including those being groomed for leadership. The bottom line is that leaders need to develop a shared understanding, shared language and shared experience of the spiritual rhythms and disciplines that lead to transformation.

FIXED-HOUR PRAYER

One of the most important aspects of our community rule of life is simply finding ways to be open to the presence of Christ. Some important questions are: How will we pray? How will we listen—to God and to each other? How will we stay faithful to the process of transformation? How will we be rested and healthy enough to bring steady, alert presence to the decisions we face? How can we remain open to Christ's presence so that he guides the process and outcomes of our decision making?

The most significant way our group has found to remain open to Christ's presence when we are together is to engage in rhythms of prayer at regular intervals throughout the day (morning, midday, evening, night) or to pray whatever "hour" is closest and most appropriate to the time we are meeting. If the meeting starts at 7 p.m. we start with Evening Prayer and close with Night Prayer. Or if it's a Saturday morning meeting, we start with Morning Prayer and end with Midday Prayer. Variously known in Christian tradition as fixed-hour prayer, praying the hours or the daily office, this approach to prayer enables us to stop at regular intervals and turn our hearts toward God in ways that are appropriate for whatever part of the day we are in.

I first participated in fixed-hour prayer on a spiritual retreat with a few like-minded souls. A member of our group had experience with fixed-hour prayer, so he prepared a simple liturgy using prayers from the Psalms, a reading from the Gospels and written prayers from the Book of Common Prayer and other prayer books. We set aside a simple prayer space and entered it in silence. We lit a candle to signify Christ's presence with us through the

Holy Spirit. Since it was evening, the prayers provided for us began with these words:

> From the rising of the sun to its setting,
> Let the name of the Lord be praised.
>
> YOU, O LORD, ARE MY LAMP.
> MY GOD, YOU MAKE MY DARKNESS BRIGHT.
>
> Light and peace in Jesus Christ our Lord.
>
> THANKS BE TO GOD.

Some of the prayers were read in unison, some responsively—and I lost myself in the beauty and simplicity of it all. Instead of having to think about what to pray, I gave myself to the beauty of words that expressed deep longings and powerful praises. Instead of getting caught up in my ego's attempts to say something profound to God (and to the people around me), I actually rested from all of that and *prayed*. Instead of listening to someone else's interpretation or application of Scripture, I heard Scripture read without comment and listened for what God was saying to me in the context of our relationship. Instead of having to endure overly stimulating programming, this small group of us settled into a silence that was rich and satisfying. I lost track of time until someone finally nudged me to remind me that it was my turn to read Scripture!

That was ten years ago, and that group (which became the Transforming Center!) has been praying that way ever since! This affinity for fixed-hour prayer came as a surprise to me. I had been raised in an evangelical tradition that was highly suspicious of so-called "rote prayers"—written prayers that we feared would foster the vain repetitions that Jesus warned about. We seemed to feel that only spontaneous prayers were real because they came from the heart. Only people who weren't spiritual and didn't have much to say to God relied on written prayers! But I have discovered another option: to pray the great prayers of the church and really mean them!

Many Protestant traditions departed from fixed-hour prayer to protest the excesses and the spiritual numbness of the Roman Catholic Church. But as it turns out, we lost a rich avenue of prayer that is rooted in Scripture and in our own tradition. Whether you call it fixed-hour prayer, the daily office or praying the divine hours, these prayers are deeply biblical; they express in stirring language great spiritual truth and deep human longing that has the potential to shape the soul. The Psalms, the Old and New Testament prayers (called canticles), and the Lord's Prayer all express the universal human experience of reaching out to God. There is no better way to *learn* to pray and to actually pray!

While I am not suggesting that we do away with spontaneous prayers—a very important aspect of the spiritual life—there are powerful benefits to fixed-hour prayer. For one thing, it relieves us of the need to figure out what to say, which can be exhausting. It seems that the farther along we get in the spiritual life, the harder it is to articulate the longings that lie beneath the surface of our lives, the intimacies of our life with God, the questions and disillusionments that leave us speechless. When our own words fail us, the well-chosen words of Scripture or the prayers from prayer books help us to express the inexpressible in ways that are deeply satisfying and that can open us to an encounter with God. During moments when we might not even known how to approach God, fixed-hour prayer shows us the way.

This, then, is the beginning of my advice: make prayer the first step in anything worthwhile that you attempt. Persevere and do not weaken in that prayer. Pray with confidence, because God, in his love and forgiveness, has counted on us as his own sons and daughters . . . at every moment of our lives, as we use the good things he has given us, we can respond to his love only by seeking to obey his will for us.

ST. BENEDICT, *PROLOGUE TO THE RULE*

THE POWER OF SCRIPTURE IN COMMUNITY

Although many of us pray the hours when we are alone, a special power is released when two or three (or more!) gather around the presence of Christ and together open our hearts to him. Furthermore, when we engage in fixed-hour prayer, we know we are praying what the church has written down and prayed for centuries; we join with millions of Christians around the world who are praying at the same time. This way of praying affirms that we are not alone and that our particular expression of community is part of a much larger reality—the communion of saints who have come before us, those who are present on the earth now and those who will come after us. Indeed, we are praying "with the church" in a way that expresses the deeper unity that transcends all our divisions—and that is no small thing!

We can also utilize Scripture in the leadership setting by engaging *lectio divina* together. In chapter two I mentioned the process of lectio divina as a private discipline, but it can also be experienced as a group. The moves are all the same, but one person guides the process: first by inviting the group into a few moments of silent preparation, and then by reading the chosen passage for each of the moves, perhaps offering a simple reminder about what individuals should listen for in each move. Each reading is followed by a moment or two of silence. After the silence the reader goes on to the next move (which keeps it primarily private), or you can go around the circle, allowing each individual to concisely state what they heard in that reading. This sharing should be limited to the briefest word or phrase. Then the leader goes on to the next move. This is not a time for discussion but for people to hear from God in Scripture and to acknowledge what they heard. (For an example of how to lead a lectio divina exercise, see the *Sacred Rhythms* DVD curriculum session three.) The group could use the lectionary readings for the week, or the leader or someone else in the group may feel led to use a certain passage not from the lectionary.

CREATING SPACE FOR THE SPIRIT

Another way to be led by the Holy Spirit relative to a particular decision is to actually create space for the Spirit by introducing time for silence. After fully discussing a particular agenda item, take time to listen to God in silence to see if God's Spirit brings to mind a Scripture that might provide needed guidance or perspective. Then assemble the group to share these Scriptures. When the group is made up of mature individuals accustomed to listening to the subtle moving of the Spirit, the Scriptures brought to the group from this time can powerfully shape the decision-making process. I have seen the Spirit lead people to different but complementary passages that open up a third way. At times the Spirit has led several people to the same passage—which can be simultaneously unnerving and exciting.

This approach requires spiritual maturity. Otherwise some might see it as an opportunity to use proof texts to support their preferred position. If group members lack discernment and self-awareness (as explained in earlier chapters), there is a danger that they might manipulate Scripture to their own ends. Use this method only if you trust the spiritual maturity of the group. Remember that you are seeking to let God speak through his Word to the issues you are facing. Therefore, you need people who are able to tell the difference between their own attempts to direct or control things and being open to the Spirit's leading.

One approach I stumbled onto recently came at one of our board retreats, and it actually came from feeling exhausted and stuck! All morning we had been talking about several issues that were distinct and yet connected in complicated ways. Coming into Midday Prayer and lunch, we were all a little tired, slightly mind-boggled and feeling the pressure to make some decisions. We were longing to hear a word from the Lord. So I asked that we take a few moments of silence in between the close of the morning session and Midday Prayer and encouraged people to use those moments as an opportunity to listen for a word from God through Scripture.

When we gathered to pray, we placed an open Bible on the altar. I suggested that when we came to the Scripture reading in the service, we remain quiet and allow anyone who had received a Scripture to read it—without comment—and then place the Bible back on the altar. Because of the caliber of the group, I knew that no one would be manipulative or heavy-handed. I trusted them to bring a Scripture that God had given them for us.

Oh, what a rich time of resting in God and with each other! It was restful because we knew we had done all we could do, and now we needed a way of trusting God to work in and through the community. It was restful because it was a way of giving up control—especially for me, the leader of the meeting. And it was a way of creating space for God to do something unexpected. So, several read Scripture. No one commented. After each reading, the person said, "This is the Word of the Lord," to which we all responded, "Thanks be to God." We concluded the brief prayer service and then went to lunch. When we reconvened our meeting, there was new clarity, focus and direction—renewed energy, even—that was related to the Scriptures God had given several of the individuals in the group. Thanks be to God!

PRACTICING REST AND RETREAT

Have you ever been a part of a meeting in which people were so tired that they made a decision just so they could go home? Have you ever participated in a decision-making process knowing that you were resorting to "sloppy desperation" just because you were exhausted? In their book, *The Power of Full Engagement*, Tony Schwartz and Jim Loehr make the point that

> energy, not time, is the fundamental currency of high performance. . . .
>
> It is not the intensity of energy and expenditure that pro-

duces burnout, impaired performance and physical breakdown, but rather the duration of expenditure without recovery. . . .

Leaders are stewards of organizational energy—in companies, organizations and even in families. They inspire or demoralize others first by how effectively they manage their own energy and next by how well they mobilize, focus, invest and renew the collective energy of those they lead.[3]

While it is expected that each person's personal rule of life includes getting adequate rest and taking regular retreats (hopefully monthly or quarterly) for the purpose of listening to God, it is also important that the rhythm of our life in leadership honors the need for rest, renewal and listening to God together. Very early in Jesus' leadership development of his disciples he guided them in experiencing sane rhythms of work and rest *together.* "Come away to a deserted place all by yourselves and rest awhile" he said (Mk 6:31). He didn't send them off to rest alone, and he didn't tell them to do it without him, as though he were somehow above it. There was something important about resting and retreating together.

The kind of retreat we are talking about here is not merely an off-site planning meeting in which we work longer than we would if we were back at the office. It is not a conference full of programmed events, noisy activity and too much information. A spiritual retreat is a time apart when we move slower, take time to rest, have extended time for solitude and silent listening, share our journeys and key learnings, eat together and enjoy one another's company. If we keep the arrangements simple and invite someone from outside the group to facilitate the experience, everyone gets to rest and be attentive to God.

Taking retreats together is probably easier, in some ways, for church boards and staff teams that live and work in close proximity. For national boards (like ours) where people fly in from different parts of the country, it is a little more expensive and complicated logistically, but it is infinitely worth it! Think carefully about what is realistic for your group. Do something before you try to do everything. While two retreats of this type a year is probably ideal, even one a year is a huge step in the right direction. When we neglect these times, we become tired and disconnected from ourselves, each other and God, and then we are back to having compromised some of our deepest values.

Disciplines of rest and retreat teach us to live within our limits, which is hard for leaders and even harder when they gather together. And yet there is something deeply spiritual about honoring our limitations and the boundaries God has given to leaders. Narcissistic leaders are always looking beyond their sphere of influence with visions of grandiosity far out of proportion to what is actually being given. Paul, great leader that he was, acknowledged that he had learned not to overstep his limits but to keep within the field that God had assigned to him (2 Cor 10:13). The field that God has given us is our bodies, our personalities, our work community, our calling. Living within our limits means living within the finiteness of who we are as individuals and as a community—(1) time and space; (2) our physical, emotional, relational and spiritual capacities; (3) our organization's stage of life; (4) the individuals who make up the organization; and (5) God's call. It means doing this and not that. It means doing this much and not more.

When we refuse to live within our limits, we wear out ourselves and those who lead with us. We compromise the quality of our relationships with God and the people around us. We compromise our effectiveness in doing those things we have been called to do. To live within our limits is to live humbly as the creature in the presence of our Creator. Only God is infinite; the rest of us need to be clear about what we are called to do and say no to everything else. Another reason why discernment is so important.

Personal Reflection

Take some time to notice (without judging) and reflect on the places in this chapter where you felt resistance (this could be feelings of disagreement, questions, impossibility) and also feelings of resonance or longing. What practices resonated with your own heart's desire for opening to God in the midst of your leadership with this group? What seemed possible or impossible? What are your questions or concerns? Be ready to share at least some part of your reflection with the group.

In Community

PRACTICING TOGETHER

Take time to reflect on your practices for opening to God together.

1. What are the practices you have in place already that help you to be open to God in the context of your leadership together? When have you experienced God's transforming, guiding presence as you have practiced these together?

2. Is there anything missing? Are there any practices described here that you feel drawn to explore together?

3. Make plans for at least trying the practices you feel drawn to.

CLOSING PRAYER

From the following pages, choose the fixed-hour prayers that correspond to the time of day when you are beginning and ending your meeting and pray them together. For instance, if you are beginning your meeting in the evening, begin with Evening Prayer and end with Night Prayer. If it is a morning meeting, begin with Morning Prayer and end with Midday Prayer.[4]

The prayers below are abbreviated portions of the prayer services we use in the Transforming Center; they are adapted from several different sources as noted. The nonitalic portions are to be read by a leader and the italic parts are to be read by the group as a response. Words in bold are merely descriptive or instructive and are not meant to be read out loud. Before you start, choose someone to read the leader portion so the rest of you can respond.

You may want to light a centrally located candle at the beginning of your prayer time as a symbol of Christ's Holy Spirit around whom you are gathered. Silence is indicated at an appropriate point in each prayer in case you would like to use your fixed-hour prayer as an opportunity to also experience silence together; one or two minutes of silence gives everyone a chance to breathe and settle into the thoughts expressed in the prayer rather than just saying the words in a perfunctory way. While praying in this manner might be a new experience for your group and might even feel a little awkward, I encourage you to try it as one concrete way of opening to the presence of Christ together. You have nothing to lose and a whole lot to gain!

MORNING PRAYER
Opening

O God, open our lips and we shall declare your praise.
(Psalm 51:15)

God said: Let there be light; and there was light.
And God saw that the light was good.
This very day the Lord has acted!

Let us rejoice!

Praise the Lord!

God's name be praised!

Prayer at the Beginning of the Day

New every morning is your love, great God of light,
And all day long you are working for good in the world.

Stir up in us desire to serve you,
To live peacefully with our neighbors,
And to devote this day to your Son, our Savior,
Jesus Christ the Lord. Amen.

Silence

Response

We praise you with joy, loving God,
For your grace is better than life itself.

You have sustained us through the darkness;
And you bless us with life in this new day.

In the shadow of your wings we sing for joy
And bless your holy name. Amen.

*   *   *

MIDDAY PRAYER

Opening

O God, make speed to save us.
O Lord, make haste to help us.

Silence

Gratitude at Midday

Accept, O Lord, our thanks and praise for all that you
have done for us.

We thank you for the splendor of the
whole creation, for the beauty of this world, for the
wonder of life, and for the mystery of love.

We thank you for the blessing of family and friends,

and for the loving care which surrounds us on every side.

We thank you for setting us at tasks
which demand our best efforts, and for leading us to
accomplishments which satisfy and delight us.

We thank you for those disappointments and failures
that lead us to acknowledge our dependence on you alone.

Above all, we thank you for your son Jesus Christ;
for the truth of his word and the example of his life;
for his steadfast obedience, by which he overcame temptation;
for his dying, through which he overcame death;
and for his rising to life again, in which we are
raised to the life of your kingdom.

All: Grant us the grace to be open to your Spirit, that we may
     know Christ and make him known;
     and through him, at all times and in all places,
     may give thanks to you in all things. Amen.

*   *   *

EVENING PRAYER
Opening

From the rising of the sun to its setting,
Let the name of the Lord be praised.

You, O Lord, are my lamp.
My God, you make my darkness bright.

Light and peace in Jesus Christ our Lord.

Thanks be to God.

Silence

Prayer

We praise and thank you, O God,

For you are without beginning and without end.

Through Christ, you created the whole world;

through Christ, you preserve it.

You made the day for the works of light

and the night for the refreshment of our minds and our bodies.

Keep us now in Christ, grant us a peaceful evening,
a night free from sin, and bring us at last to eternal life.
Through Christ and in the Holy Spirit,

we offer you all glory, honor and worship,

now and forever. *Amen.*

*   *   *

NIGHT PRAYER
Opening

Our souls greet you, Shepherd God.

We have been led by your loving hand,
and we proclaim with joy that you are our salvation.

Reign in our hearts this night.

Amen.

Prayer

For thus says the Lord God, the Holy One of Israel:

in returning and rest you shall be saved;
in quietness and in trust shall be your strength.

Therefore the Lord waits to be gracious to you;
Therefore he will rise up to show mercy to you.

For the Lord is a God of justice;
blessed are all those who wait for him.

Amen.

Silence

Benediction

Sovereign God, you have been our help during the day
and you promise to be with us at night.

Receive this prayer as a sign of our trust in you.
Save us from all evil, keep us from harm,
and guide us in your way. We belong to you, Lord.
Protect us by the power of your name,
in Jesus Christ, we pray. Amen.[5]

7

PRACTICES FOR LISTENING
TO EACH OTHER

*There is nothing more hurtful than to try to love one another
and not knowing how to do it intelligently.*

GORDON COSBY

❧

The staff and elders of Grace Church were a little overwhelmed
by all the possibilities for putting in place practices that would
help them open to God in their meetings and interactions. Their
hearts were also deeply stirred. They realized that their meetings
were usually very businesslike and not all that different from
secular meetings. There was always a lot of good-natured banter
and joking, but nothing that was intentionally designed to help
them seek God together.

Their facilitator encouraged the different teams to begin by
picking one thing they thought they could put in place just to get
started. The staff felt that since they all worked together, they
would start every day with Morning Prayer. They also wanted to at
least try starting meetings with a few moments of silence before

jumping into the agenda. Since the elders met on Tuesday nights, they decided to start their meetings with Evening Prayer. They also decided to use the lectionary Gospel reading for that week so no one would have to make the decision about what Scripture to read.

They were very excited about opening to God in this way, but they also knew that they needed practices that would help them open to each other. Some of the ways they related to each other were not very productive and were even hurtful at times. As the church had grown and the pastor had become more well-known— a local celebrity of sorts—there was less accountability. He had a tendency to spin truth to get things to go his way, and the rest of the staff was afraid to disagree or point out any discrepancies they might notice. Since he was the only staff member who attended elders meetings, the rest of the staff weren't sure they were getting the straight scoop, and there was some nervousness about how they were being represented to the elders. It was not an environment conducive to truth telling.

The pastor didn't feel all that safe either. He had a sense that the other elders sometimes talked behind his back and that they came into meetings having already lobbied for each other's support. A couple of the elders could not handle conflict, so when there were strong disagreements, they shut down emotionally and sometimes even left the room. As a result, there were several conflicts that had never been fully resolved. People just soldiered on, pretending things were okay and trying to avoid the land mines buried in their shared history. They always felt slightly on edge and that they needed to be careful. On top of that, no one ever repented for anything; if something went wrong in a meeting—an angry outburst, an unnecessary criticism, a person getting cut off or dismissed—no one ever apologized. They just came to the next meeting and pretended nothing had happened. Clearly, these communication patterns were not going to take them where they wanted to go.

CONNECTING AT THE SOUL LEVEL

Leadership discernment requires us to be open and receptive to God *with each other* and to be open and receptive to each other *with God*. This is a much more vulnerable stance than most of us are willing to take in leadership settings. The truth is, most leadership groups are not safe enough for those present to offer the wisdom that comes only from being in touch with what is truest within them. A commitment to leadership discernment requires cultivating an environment in which it is safe for people to speak from their heart and soul, not just their mind.

When I use the term *soul*, I am referring to the essence of a person—the true self as created in the image of God. Although it is easy to think of the physical body and the material world as "real," the truth is that the soul—the place where God is present to us and where God's Spirit witnesses with our spirit about things that are true (Rom 8:16)—is equally real, spiritually speaking. The soul is a person's core self or spiritual center where the physical, mental and emotional life come together as one in relation to God. This is the part of each of us that our leadership group most needs.

We need to choose whether we will relate to one another and make decisions based on external considerations alone or whether we will cultivate an environment in which the soul—our true self *in* God and responsive *to* God—can be fully engaged in the discernment process. A community that exists to discern and do the will of God must be a place where people can freely offer what they are in touch with *at that level*. This kind of environment does not develop by accident; it is cultivated intentionally through trustworthy relational practices that make it safe for the soul to fully engage with other souls in God's presence.

As each practice is described, you will have the opportunity to personally reflect on the importance of that particular relational practice for you. Then you will talk about it as a group. Is this something the group is already practicing? If so, how important is it relative to your own soul's willingness to say true things? If not, does the absence of that practice have a positive or negative impact on your ability to speak from the soul? Would you be willing to commit to this practice in the context of your leadership group?

PRACTICING TRANSFORMATION

The practice associated with the value of spiritual transformation is establishing a rule of life (as we described earlier). In a community that values transformation, anyone in leadership should be able to articulate a regular pattern of spiritual practices, attitudes and behaviors that keep them open and available to God. They should be just as clear about their spiritual rhythms as they are about their eating, sleeping and exercise habits.

As part of your shared commitment to transformation, you could incorporate a rhythm of checking in with each other about how you are experiencing God's transforming presence in the context of each person's personal rule of life. (Hopefully, people would have something pretty current to say!)

> ### *Personal Reflection*
> *Do you have a rule of life? If not, begin sketching a few core commitments that will help you to practice transformation.*

PRACTICING LOVE

Whatver else we are seeking to discern about God's will, we can be sure that God wants us to love each other. And the outcome of spiritual transformation is an increasing capacity to love God and love others, which can be measured in concrete ways. In order for community to be sustained at any level of human relating, our commitment to love—not as an emotion but as a set of attitudes, behaviors and concrete actions—must be primary. This simple truth easily gets lost in the press of organizational or congregational life.

For Christians there is no adequate measure of our success at discerning and doing God's will outside of our commitment to love one another. We can do many wonderful, altruistic, strategic things, but if we are not loving each other in the midst of it all, our accomplishments are empty from the standpoint of spiritual integrity. As a group gets caught up in its mission, we can find ourselves moving slowly (almost imperceptibly at first) from serving people to using them for our own ends, from loving people to being impatient with and harsh toward them, from trusting them to eyeing them with suspicion and fear. By the time we notice how far we have drifted from this basic Christian value, we are in dangerous waters! So, when a community comes together to do the will of God, the first step is loving one another—not in theory but in practice. This is not to be confused with the shallow and debilitating understanding of love that prevails in our culture. Robert Mulholland notes, "The kind of love that sustains Christian community is agape—the radical, other-referenced, non-self-centered mode of being revealed most profoundly in God as cruciform love."[1]

So what are the concrete expressions of agape in a leadership environment? At the very least it means we are taking time to listen to each other, to demonstrate kindness in word and deed, and to pray for one another when together or apart. As we work and lead together, we value each other and affirm each other's gifts and unique contributions to the body of Christ (Rom 12; 1 Cor 12). When there is misunderstanding or hurt in a particular relationship, when there is resistance to a particular direction taken, we create time and space to pay attention because unity is Christ's will and longing for us. We are committed to graciously telling the truth to each other—even when that truth is challenging—because honesty is deeply honoring to persons and relationships. In short, *we value people and the quality of our relationships as they relate to agape more than programs or products.*

One of the greatest accomplishments of Jesus' time on earth (and one that he reported to his heavenly Father) was that "he loved [his own] to the end" (Jn 13:1). If we fail to love with the cruciform love that Christ so powerfully demonstrated, we have truly failed.

> ### *Personal Reflection*
> *One of the most confounding aspects of leadership is how people understand and express love differently. What one person feels is a loving behavior can be threatening to or completely misunderstood by another. What actions and behavior help you feel loved and valued in a group?*

PRACTICING STABILITY

Stability is an interesting practice for us Protestants who are most accustomed to leaving our communities when the going gets tough, starting another denomination when we disagree over doctrine or practice, and shopping for a church like we shop for a house—only it seems we leave our churches more frequently than we leave our houses these days!

In the monastic tradition the vow of stability is central to a rule of life. The person promises to remain in that particular monastic community for life and to be shaped by the rhythms of that particular community. This commitment is understood as laying down one's life *in its entirety*, placing it in the hands of God.

> The vow of stability is the first of the vows because nothing is possible until we give our entire life to the primacy of God's kingdom. If we leave ourselves an escape hatch, we have one foot out the door and we are not fully committed. If we say to ourselves that we will stay committed as long as commitment stays exciting and devoid of suffering, we are not fully committed. . . . The grass is not greener "over there": one must work out one's problems with *this* person because if one doesn't, one will have to work it out with *that* person. This is precisely what

is so freeing about the vow of stability . . . to have to work it out is to demand growth, as painful as it is, and that is freeing. Faithfulness is a limit that forces us to stop running and encounter God, self, and other right now, right here.[2]

Lord have mercy! This is just not the kind of commitment most Protestants are accustomed to. In fact, many church polities don't even allow for this much stability at the leadership level. Leaders rotate off boards at predetermined intervals. Thus groups are never together long enough to get traction on their commitment to each other in community, to really settle in to all that stability means and then to reap the benefits of having been shaped together by shared practices. Sometimes it seems that when everyone has reached a place of trust and is functioning optimally out of shared commitment, it's time for some to leave and others to come on.

While I can certainly appreciate that there are good reasons for rotating terms, it doesn't provide the opportunity for stable, long-term community at the leadership level. And love doesn't grow well in a garden of uncertainty. What is the best way for us to experience stability in community at the leadership level?

When stability is experienced in one's commitment to the church or community, and that community is cultivating trust and transformation as group norms, anyone who serves in a leadership role has been shaped by those norms and can fit right in. When different members are called upon to serve the larger community in a leadership capacity, group norms keep the leadership group functioning consistently.

It can be good to create a nonvoting position on the board that allows people who have rotated off to still be present to contribute as discerners, as pray-ers or as sages. This allows them to take a break but to also remain engaged in the community life of the group. This way, the group doesn't lose everything they have worked so hard to achieve with each other.

In the Transforming Center we do not have predetermined terms of service for our leadership community because the benefits to stability in our relationships at that level seem to far outweigh the disadvantages. Our commitment to stability is that we commit to stay together until together we discern a need for change. This is our way of creating stability in our relationships while at the same time leaving room for the will of God to be revealed among us.

We cannot demand this kind of stability of others; we can only offer it as a true invitation of the spiritual life. Stability is a powerful invitation—to transformation, to creativity, to long-term impact. As Brian Taylor points out,

> It is the failure to commit oneself entirely that blocks creativity in the spiritual life, in the artistic life, in the relational life. Meeting one's obligations with a minimum of commitment may seem like freedom, but it enslaves us to what is fleeting. . . . In the instability of our age we are constantly reassessing the self—our direction and purpose, our commitments and values. Without the constancy of stability, this assessment can create chaos. Ultimately, the vow of stability is a vow of stability to God. God is the only true eternal rock upon which we can stand. But God calls us into a particular life, to be spent in the company of particular people, . . . to accept one's life as it is given is to begin to find freedom.[3]

Personal Reflection

What appeals to you about stability? What resistance do you have?

SUBMITTING TO DISCERNMENT

Something that continually surprises me is that after committing to discernment together, people often continue to make significant decisions—moving to another state, taking another job and even starting another ministry—without engaging the group they are a part of! I have often scratched my head in absolute amazement and wondered, *What did they think we were talking about when we talked about discerning God's will together on important matters that affect the group?*

One of the reasons for this failure to discern important matters togther may be that the commitment to discernment runs so counter to the independent mindset of our Western culture. It literally doesn't compute that one would confer with others regarding what seems like a personal decision. For instance, the decision to move or to take another job may seem like a personal decision, and yet it affects the whole group and warrants at least some willingness to discern together. If we are part of a group cultivated as a community for discernment and we say that we respect one another on that level, what does it mean if we choose *not* to lean into that group when we are seeking a greater understanding of God's will for our lives? It is quite disillusioning to such a group to find out that members are just doing their own thing anyway.

While we might be quick to jump on the discernment bandwagon because it is certainly very attractive from a spiritual standpoint (what Christian doesn't want to be known as being committed to discerning the will of God?), when the stakes are high we are not sure we want to submit to the wisdom and discernment of a group. Maybe it's that we don't trust each other, we don't trust God, or we don't trust the process. Perhaps it's some combination of all three. Sometimes I wonder if it is just plain willfulness. Whatever it is, we need to talk not only about whether we *value* discernment but also about whether we are willing to really *practice* it. The group needs to agree on the kinds of decisions we are committed to bringing to the group.

Discernment includes the commitment to consider all pertinent factual data *and* to honor inner dynamics such as consolation and desolation (see chapter three), fear and resistance, desire and calling. As individuals enter more deeply into the process of spiritual transformation and become more discerning, our awareness of these inner dynamics will become more pronounced. When left unacknowledged or when there is no way to process them, they can cause people to behave strangely or even badly. They might withdraw emotionally or give in to "fight or flight" reactions, self-protective strategies, manipulation, passive-aggressive behaviors and so on. When fear is not acknowledged, it can cause us to shrink back without even considering the fact that perhaps God is calling us to confront our fears and move forward in faith.

If we are willing to pay attention, the presence of fear can alert us to situations that are truly dangerous so we can respond in several different ways: (1) exercise wisdom and ask, *Is there real danger here? Is there something in the person's resistance to pay attention to?* (2) hear God's challenge for us to be courageous, or (3) pay attention to areas where our trust in God or each other is weak and needs to be strengthened.

The same is true of desolation. When someone among us experiences desolation regarding a decision the rest of the group feels good about, this can be a wonderful opportunity to slow down the momentum and listen for the wisdom contained in that person's gut reaction. If the person hangs back and does not feel free to share, important wisdom might be missed! If the person does not feel that such inner dynamics will be heard and respected, he or she may drag his or her feet or in other ways subtly resist the direction the group is headed, which will only cause frustration and feelings of dis-ease.

Personal Reflection

What kinds of decisions (both personal and corporate) do you feel warrant discernment with the group?

PRACTICING TRUTH TELLING

Truth telling is the spiritual practice associated with valuing truth, and it is essential to life in community. Knowing that group members function with immaculate integrity expressed through a tenacious commitment to truth telling is a foundational building block of trustful relationships. So foundational, in fact, that "not bearing false witness" was one of the Ten Commandments given to the children of Israel to help them navigate the perils of their wilderness journey together.

Gareth Icenogle describes truth telling as central to the process of developing mutual trust in community.

Community only grows in the presence of truth. . . .

Small groups are only as strong as the group's ability to develop mutual trust. . . .

The sharing of truth sustains the group into the advanced stages [of group life] as deeper and deeper patterns of intimacy are experienced. The avoidance of truth breaks the growing trust patterns. This can open a dark door to distrust and move the group into a period of unrest until the truth is reestablished through confrontation, confession and forgiveness. Sustained periods of unrest and avoidance of truth will cause even the strongest of groups to disintegrate. This disintegration is the result of trying to live without the delicate marriage of truth with intimacy. Truth cannot be shared without intimacy, and intimacy cannot be sustained without truth. Truth, love and justice must all work together in group life.[4]

It's important that leaders talk about the role of truth telling in the leadership community, not just because it is morally right but also as a concrete discipline that we are committed to practicing together. In a church culture increasingly influenced by secular leadership models that are more concerned with *spinning* the truth than *telling* the truth, knowing what this commitment means *to us specifically* is critical. When any expression of Christ's church sees itself more as a corporation than as a community, it is easy to rationalize degrees of truth telling. What might be acceptable in a secular workplace environment (although this is arguable) is not good for relationships between brothers and sisters gathered round the presence of Christ. It is important to be clear about what truth telling means to us in practice.

Personal Reflection

The following scenarios raise questions about what it means (and how challenging it actually is) to practice truth telling in a leadership setting—even those that involve employment. Take some time to reflect on them personally.

- You are serving with people you love and trust in a high-level staff position in a church or Christian organization. You know that your contributions are highly valued and significant to the ministry. You are approached by another group to consider working for them, and they ask you to meet with them about this employment opportunity while you are at a conference with your current colleagues. Do you hide what's going on until it's a done deal? At what point do you share honestly about this new situation? What does your commitment to trustworthiness, truth telling and discernment in community mean in a situation like this?

- You have serious concerns about certain aspects of your senior leader's character or leadership style. In fact, you are angry about certain things that have happened or your perception of what has happened. In fact, you have gotten so fed up that you are thinking of quitting or resigning. What does commitment to truth telling require? Do you quit without saying anything about what is bothering you or do you say it is about something else? Do you talk to others in the group about it? Do you speak directly with that person and share the whole truth? Can the group handle talking about it together? What is your commitment to each other as individuals and to the group relative to truth telling in this type of situation?

- There has been a serious moral failure in your community—either someone in your leadership group or in some other level of leadership. What is your commitment to "speaking the truth in love"—to the person(s) involved, to each other in the leadership community and also to the congregation or constituency? How do the values of truth telling and confidentiality fit together?

- You have a question or an observation about some aspect of the character or relationship patterns of one of your colleagues in leadership, or someone else has an observation or question and shares it with you. What does a commitment to truth telling call you to?

- Something is not going very well in some aspect of the ministry—it could be anything from dwindling numbers to low offerings to an unresolved conflict between staff members. This is having a negative effect on the staff. The senior pastor or CEO is a very high-powered, bottom-line-oriented person who reacts badly to this kind of news and tends to shoot the messenger. Over the years, unspoken rules have developed that dictate what kind of truth does and does not get shared with senior leadership; an inordinate amount of energy and conversation revolves around determining exactly how to frame or spin the truth. What do you do with this important news that has come to light? How could a more concrete and open commitment to truth telling shift this pattern in the culture? What would it take?

Take time to talk about each one of these scenarios. Don't discuss these as case studies but as situations that could happen in your work together. Maybe they already have! Allow these scenarios to lead you to clarify specific commitments you want to make to each other regarding telling the truth to each other. Commitments such as, *When something is going on in our lives that will significantly affect the rest of the group, we will be forthcoming rather than hiding it from the group.* Or *If one of us observes something or is angered by something another person does, we will speak to that person directly; we will not talk about it with others. If we can't resolve it on our own, we will bring it openly and honestly to the group for help and guidance.* Keep on developing your list until everyone can affirm that there is enough of a commitment to truth telling that they will risk telling the whole truth when that is what's needed.

In a healthy group, any person in the group can call the group back to its commitment to truth telling if and when that commitment is violated. Remember to *affirm* each other every time someone tells the truth—even when it's hard—for the good of the group. When someone brings to the group a truth that is difficult or challenging, before anyone says anything else in response, affirm that person along these lines: "Thank you for taking the risk to tell us the truth. Truth telling is hard and you have served us by bringing us this truth. Even though this is hard to hear, we are truly grateful."

PRACTICING CONFESSION

We live in a culture that promotes a profound sense of denial about the sin in our lives and the way our sin wounds others and impacts the groups we are a part of. It is a natural tendency of human nature—seen clearly when things went wrong in the Garden of Eden—to pin the blame on others rather than taking responsibility for ourselves. We are much more prone (and even encouraged) to go to great lengths to avoid owning our stuff, or to at least soften it to make it seem less significant than it is. The scriptural instruction "confess your sins to one another, and pray for one another, so that you may be healed" (Jas 5:16) is profoundly countercultural for most leadership settings. Instead, we are much more accustomed to putting our best and most polished foot forward. Confession runs counter to human nature as well and yet it is profoundly hopeful! If we are willing to engage in the practice of confession, it is possible for us to be healed in relation to one another and to limit the effects of sin in our gatherings so that Christ's purposes can go forward unhindered.

Confession is the culmination of our personal practice of self-examination. It leads to increasing self-awareness, which increases the health and functionality of our life together in community. Healthy self-examination and confession is the process of *seeing* something that went wrong in an attitude, behavior or action, and how it affected (or affects) our presence and behavior in the group. Then there is the willingness to *name it* for what it is and also name what was going on inside us, seeking some understanding of the inner dynamics that caused this behavior. At first, this may happen after the fact, but as we become more practiced, we can actually have this kind of awareness in the moment. Better yet, we might become aware of it in enough time to reign in potentially bad behavior.

In this process, we may need to ask God to guide us in noticing the inner wounds, character deficiencies or sin patterns that caused or tempted us to bad behavior. This brings about a kind of awakening in which we see ourselves more clearly in God's presence, we are able to confess and ask forgiveness, and we open ourselves to God's cleansing and purifying work in our lives. This is the practice of personal confession.

When we are part of a leadership group, it is important that we also cultivate the practice of corporate confession. This can be a commitment to general confession as part of our prayer practice (confession is often a part of Night Prayer) as well as to confessing our sins privately to those directly affected and to the group if our behavior has affected others. I know of one pastor who, after becoming convicted about his pace of life, actually confessed this to his staff, acknowledging that it had been harmful to him and to them. He asked their forgiveness and shared with them concrete ways he intended to change in his personal life and in their life together.

Confession, when practiced fully, is *personal* (between God and me, and sometimes a trusted friend or confessor), it is *interpersonal* (with the person or persons I have offended), and it is *corporate* (in the context of community and our prayers together). It is the interplay between these three that keeps confession healthy and productive. Healthy functioning in community is dependent not only on our growing self-awareness but also our ability to take responsibility for the quality of our presence and action in the group by acknowledging and confessing sin. In the prayer at the conclusion of this chapter there is an opportunity for confession. If your group is ready, pause after the confession and give everyone the opportunity to confess sins that have affected the group and to receive God's forgiveness.

Personal Reflection

Have you ever had an experience of corporate confession in a leadership setting? What was that like? What impact did it have on the group and its ability to function in a healthy way?

PRACTICING CONFLICT TRANSFORMATION

It is one thing to believe in the *idea* of being open to the transforming presence of Christ when we are in the midst of conflict; it is quite another to actually practice it! Usually when we find ourselves in the middle of a conflict, our emotions highjack rational thought, our defenses go up, and a whole set of primal fears kick in.

It doesn't matter how much we agree with Matthew 18 or how many times we have taught it, everything in us resists actually doing it. And *that*, my friends, is why we need a practice. While describing a fully-orbed approach to conflict transformation is beyond the scope of this book, there are several practices that will help us with the challenges and potential gifts contained in human conflict.

Conflict transformation begins with at least two shared affirmations. First, *we affirm Jesus' promise to be with us in the midst of conflict and find ways to open to his presence in it.* This might include

- agreeing on a particular way of praying
- helpful opening and closing rituals
- taking time for silence at key points in the conversation
- becoming aware of our breathing as a way of quieting primitive fight-or-flight impulses
- framing the conversation in terms of seeking to understand the demands of Christian love in this situation
- committing ourselves to remain open to God and to the other person even when everything in us wants to shut down

Second, *we affirm that conflict can be the catalyst for needed growth and transformation for everyone involved* if we are willing to engage it as such. We are willing to engage conflict not only for the purpose of resolving the conflict but also for the purpose of continuing our own process of transformation. We give dealing with the conflicts among us the highest level of priority and attention as an expression of our love for Jesus, who desires our unity and oneness, and as a testimony to a watching world (Jn 17).

With these affirmations clearly in mind, *we commit to direct, face-to-face communication rather than resorting to triangulation and speaking behind each other's backs* (Mt 18:15). If one-on-one communication doesn't bring the needed resolution, *we are committed to involving an objective third party who is trusted by each person involved* (especially if there are power dynamics involved), knowing that the presence of others can help us listen (Mt 18:16). *We are committed to increasing self-awareness through the practice of self-examination* in relation to the conflict; we seek to maintain the willingness to allow God to show us our part in the conflict and to make confession as needed (Jas 5:16). *We are committed to discerning and doing God's will in the midst of conflict*, making it our highest priority to seek a greater understanding of what God is doing so we can join God in it (Acts 15). *We will be proactive in developing skills and practices related to conflict transformation* and articulating those clearly for the group.

Personal Reflection

How do you respond to the idea of making these commitments to conflict transformation?

As painful as it is to acknowledge, Matthew 18 also alerts us to the reality that there may be situations in which the offending party will not enter into conflict transformation and refuses to listen or respond to the community as it calls for reconciliation. Scripture is clear that such a person must be removed from fellowship for the health and well-being of the community. Although we need to be careful about how we carry this out, part of the shepherding function of those in leadership is being prepared to make the hard call when it is necessary.

Intense conflict is an invitation to turn to God, who wants to lead us forward into restored relationships and into new organizational processes.

JAN WOOD, LON FENDALL AND BRUCE BISHOP,
PRACTICING DISCERNMENT TOGETHER

A COMMUNITY FOR DISCERNMENT

Spiritual community requires more than our minds and our intellect; it requires us to engage with heart and soul. It requires more than Robert's Rules of Order; it requires time and space for opening to God together. It requires more than collegiality, it requires love and deep relational commitment. It requires more than good intentions; it requires practice.

When we come together as a community for discernment, we do whatever we need to do to cultivate the qualities that move us toward the goal of being transformed so that we can discern and do the will of God. We establish spiritual practices that open us to God and relational practices that create a safe place for our souls to show up with each other. We proactively cultivate those values and practices which promote community and we are vigilant in recognizing and rejecting those behaviors that do not contribute to our life together in community. It's pretty much that simple.

In Community

PRACTICING TOGETHER

This chapter describes only the most basic relational disciplines that create a safe environment for leadership discernment. You will need to add others that are important to your group, but you can at least start the process by taking time to discuss those described here using the reflection exercises. The outcome of this chapter is to identify the *relational* practices that all agree are important and to which you intend to commit yourselves. Feel free to add others or to discuss in more detail the way you want to practice them. Discuss the following practices together.

- *Transformation.* Take time as a group to find out if each person has a rule of life in place and how they are experiencing God in that context. (If some don't have a rule of life, encourage them to clarify their commitment to "practicing transformation" by establishing such a rhythm.) Craft a personal rule of life as part of your commitment *to each other*—to do whatever it takes to bring a transforming self into the leadership setting.

- *Love.* Discuss what it would look like for you to love each other as you lead together. What will your commitment be? Allow time for each individual to share what makes them feel loved and valued so you can love each other intelligently rather than hoping to stumble into it by accident.

- *Stability.* Even though you are probably not a monastic community, take some time to talk about the importance of stability in relationships and what stability might look like for your leadership group. What difference would it make? What are you willing to commit yourselves to in this regard?

- *Discernment.* If your group has gotten this far, it can probably be assumed that you are committed to the value of discernment, but now take some time to discuss how you will practice this in concrete ways. What kinds of decisions (both personal and corporate) do you agree warrant discernment with the group? Can each of you commit to bringing these kinds of things to the group? How well does your group do at paying attention and processing inner dynamics such as fear and resistance, desire and calling, consolation and desolation? How will you demonstrate respect for the inner dynamics that take place within the souls of spiritual people? How will you create space for paying attention to them?

- *Truth telling.* Turn back to the scenarios on pages 141-42. Allow yourselves to fully enter into each of the scenarios as a way of clarifying what your commitment to truth telling with each other actually means. This commitment needs to come from inside each person rather than simply being imposed from the outside. Talk about these scenarios together.

- *Confession.* What is the desire and willingness of the group to practice confession? How might you incorporate confession into your patterns of being and leading together?

- *Conflict transformation.* How do you feel about making the proposed commitments on pages 146-47 in how you handle conflict?

After you have worked your way through the practices described in this chapter, you might want to wrap up your discussion by asking, Is there any other practice that seems necessary or important to us as we seek to cultivate a leadership community where we can relate to one another on the soul level? Then choose someone to lead you in this closing prayer. The nonitalic portions are read by the leader, and the italicized parts are read by all.

CLOSING PRAYER
O Trinity of love,
God in community,
Holy and One,
look now on us who look to you.

And hear our prayer for our community:

Where there is falseness

smother it by your truth

Where there is any coldness

kindle it with your love

Where there is joy and hope

free us to share it together

And make us one

as you are one.

Before God and you who are near me,

I release anything I hold against you;
I regret all I have done to harm you;
I stand beside the wrong in my life
[pause for spoken confession]
and ask for God's forgiveness.

Before God and you who are near
we release anything we hold
against one another;
we regret all the harm we have done;
we stand beside the wrong in our lives
[pause for spoken confession]
and we ask God's forgiveness.

Jesus says to us, each one:
"Go and sin no more,
come and follow me."
Now bind us together in honesty
As we pray the prayer that Jesus taught us:

Our Father in heaven,
hallowed be your name;
your kingdom come, your will be done,
on earth as it is in heaven.
Give us today our daily bread.
forgive us our sins
as we forgive those who sin against us.
Save us in the time of trial
and deliver us from evil.
for the kingdom, the power and the glory
are yours,
now and for ever. Amen.[5]

8

A Covenant That Protects Community

Intimate relationships among members of a community take time.
We need to call upon our faith: covenant is achieved by the action
of the Holy Spirit freeing people, giving them
a sense of trust with each other.

John English

❧

The Grace Church group had been completely enlivened by their conversation about practices they could do together that would help them open up to God and become more trustworthy with each other in the context of ministry. For the first time in a long time they felt hopeful about what the quality of their lives and relationships could be like. And they felt like they were getting in touch with a deeper and more spiritual dynamic of ministry than they had touched in a long time. So they were surprised when their facilitator brought up the idea of creating a covenant out of the guiding values and practices they had discussed and agreed upon.

"Why a covenant?" they wondered. "Aren't we all mature Christians; don't we know how to behave Christianly with each other? After all, we've talked and prayed about guiding values and principles. We've agreed on some practices we want to do together. Isn't that enough?"

They were shocked when their facilitator answered this question with an emphatic no!

KEEPIN' IT REAL

Discussing guiding values and transforming practices and feeling good about them doesn't mean people will choose them or stick with them when the journey gets long or the going gets tough. I've seen "mature" Christians commit slander and talk behind each other's backs. I've witnessed anger among Christian leaders that could rival anything we might expect to see in a secular environment (though perhaps thinly veiled with spiritual language or rationale). I've known committed Christians who have left churches and organizations in anger, refusing to practice Jesus' admonitions found in Matthew 18, and leaders who have refused to engage in a reconciliation process even when asked for one.

Some Christian leaders simply cannot endure the honest truth—whether it's an important truth they need to tell or a truth someone needs to tell them. I've heard of Christian boards that have held secret meetings to oust their leader. I've seen Christians hold other Christians hostage through passive-aggressive behavior without even knowing what they were doing. I know long-time church members who seem incapable of deeper self-awareness or taking responsibility for their own negative behaviors. Even if they are sometimes able to acknowledge their negative patterns, they are unable to change because they are not ready to relinquish their false-self patterns.

So—why do we need a covenant? Because *a written covenant makes our commitment real on a level that mere conversation does not.* It provides a way for the group to claim shared ownership for their behavior because it contains detailed guidelines that help the group function together in agreed-upon ways. Without an actual covenant or written agreement, a group may not be clear about what they have agreed on, let alone what it means in the context of day-to-day life in leadership community. Something this important cannot be left up to chance or wishful thinking. Spiritual community is so tender and fragile that it requires some protective structures in order for it to survive. When we are tempted to revert to old, unredeemed patterns, our covenant can call us back to our best intentions.

COVENANT: AN EXPRESSION OF GOD'S NATURE

A covenant is an agreement two or more people make with each other about how they will behave in their relationship. It protects the relationships most precious to us or in which we are most vulnerable. Marriage vows, ordination to pastoral ministry, the Hippocratic Oath and monastic vows are good examples. These types of relationships contain such potential for good and are so foundational to our well-being (and in some cases our survival) that it is worth risking ourselves to them, but we also want to establish parameters that will both protect us and help us to succeed in that relationship. We put covenants in place when what is at stake is so important that we dare not leave the relationship up to chance, subject to passing whims or confused by misunderstanding.

The word *covenant* comes from the word *convene*, which has to do with bringing persons together. Covenant making and covenant keeping are rooted in who God is. It is God's nature to be in relationship (God exists forever as a community of three). And even a cursory reading of Scripture illuminates how central covenant making and covenant keeping are to God's self-expression. In Scripture we see descriptions of covenant relationships God initiated with Noah, Abraham, Moses and David. In the New Testament God makes a new covenant with his people through the blood of Christ. Clearly, God does not enter into significant relationships without making a covenant.

God's pattern is to make covenants with individuals on behalf of a group. His covenants are made with groups who are willing to follow God in intentional ways toward a God-ordained vision. God's covenant with Abraham, for example, was *for the purpose of* creating a "great nation" through whom "all the families of the earth shall be blessed" (Gen 12:1-3). This was a call to be in community *with* God and to become a community *for* the benefit of others.

Making and keeping covenants is the way God does relationships.

> God makes covenants with groups so that individuals and relationships will be held accountable to grow and to be better within the group so their life together can have a positive effect on the wider culture and world. The Ten Commandments are a primary example of human covenant life being ordered by faith in a living and loving God. These commandments point to the need for a group to give God and humanity their full dignity in relationship and in community. . . . The Ten Commandments, when practiced, helped the group participate in God's covenantal life. When ignored, the group degenerated farther into chaos and anarchy, into non-community.[1]

COVENANT MAKING AS A SPIRITUAL PRACTICE

A group's willingness to covenant together around shared values and practices gives definition to its commitment to follow God together. There is something about entering into a covenant relationship that reflects who God is and forms a more Christlike character within us. Our commitment to a healthy covenant life is not just a commitment to each other; it is a covenant with God himself to live with each other in the way God has ordained. Since our God is a convening God, one who brings people together for God's purposes, we are participating in God's nature and character when we covenant with each other.

A covenant gives shape and form to our togetherness around a shared purpose. It is a binding and solemn agreement made by two or more individuals to do or not to do specific things on our way to a common destination. Our commitment to healthy covenant life is grounded in God's love and personal presence; through agreed-upon practices we seek to be open and responsive to that presence in and through our relationships with each other. The Ten Commandments illustrate this dual priority: the first four commandments direct our relationship with God; the remaining six have to do with our relationship with each other. Our covenant is, first of all, a covenant with God. Before God *and* with the people of God we make certain commitments regarding how we will honor God, each other and our relationships as brothers and sisters in the family of God. If we break this covenant, we dishonor not only each other but God himself.

This is very sobering. But it is also life-giving because when we make a covenant before God in relation to each other and seek to be faithful to that covenant, it can become a source of grace. Making and keeping a covenant actually becomes a spiritual practice that opens us to God's transforming presence.

Personal Reflection

What is your previous experience with covenant making and keeping? In your experience, what is its value? What are the challenges? How do you feel about making a covenant with your leadership community?

LIKE A FETTER

At a recent conference, Jeff Greenway, former president of Asbury Seminary, explained the meaning of *covenant* in a way that is particularly illuminating. He pointed out that the Hebrew word translated "covenant" comes from the word *fetter,* which means to bind, shackle or chain. While this may seem a little harsh to our contemporary Western minds, the application Jeff made was very helpful. He said,

"We bind ourselves to each other in times of strength so that in moments of weakness we do not become unbound."

How true! When we first consider establishing guiding values and principles and allow ourselves to dream of practicing spiritual disciplines together in more than just a perfunctory way, it is inspiring. I remember presenting this idea to our own leadership community and describing a few of the values and practices that we were already living and could consider formalizing. In response, some were almost euphoric, affirming their desire to move forward in this way: "This is the kind of leadership experience I've been waiting for all my life!" Others acknowledged that they were "hoping against hope" that this was indeed possible. Their hearts resonated with it, but after what they had experienced in other leadership settings, they weren't sure if they could trust that it was possible. Still others expressed their hopes and dreams that we could actually live this way.

I was glad for people's positive response, but I also took it with a grain of salt because, having led this kind of process before, I knew how challenging it can be to live our values as the realities of the journey set in. When we are faced with a decision that requires discernment and everything in us screams to make the decision ourself, when someone in the group is experiencing consolation or desolation and we are too busy or too annoyed to pay attention, when there is relational dis-ease or even conflict and we would rather talk about it with others than go directly to that person, when there is truth that is hard to say and we would rather not say it, when we know there is something in ourselves that is not quite right and is hampering our ability to be a discerning presence in the group but we don't want to face it—we realize how demanding living in covenant community is, and we might wish there was an easier way!

We cannot assume that Christian people agree on what it means to act Christianly, let alone that they are psychologically and spiritually healthy enough to carry out the agreed-on behaviors. We cannot assume that people agree on what it means to be a community. Or if they do, we cannot assume their level of commitment to it without clarifying what we are committed *to* and giving opportunity to *verbalize that commitment together.* Even though it is tempting to skip the step of creating a written covenant, don't do it! Finish the process of establishing your "rule of life" in community by articulating guiding values and principles, agreeing on the practices that will help you live your values and the rhythm in which you will practice them. *This is the content of your covenant.*

Don't feel you need to do it all at once. Along with other values and practices that you have already clarified, start by affirming what you are already doing that is working. Agree on some practices that will help you live those values. You can always add more later and provide nuance as you go. Start documenting what you know and then make a covenant—agree together—that this is indeed how you intend to live and lead together. You will never regret the time and effort you give to this process. Chances are, you may even wish you had spent more!

> Early in its life a group's members will do well to create explicit covenants. Operating on an implicit covenant will eventually result in some sort of impasse. The group will break down in conflict, wander in uncertainty, climb all over one another, and take an exorbitant amount of time dealing with internal matters. Establishing a clear covenant empowers each person in the group.[2]

UNDERSTANDING THE PROCESS

Establishing guiding values and principles, and creating a covenant around them, is not primarily an intellectual activity or brainstorming session. It is a tender, God-breathed, God-guided process that requires individuals to listen to their deepest longings and bring their most intimate truth to the table. It involves listening to the life and calling, successes and failures of the group, and learning from them. It involves letting God show you where you are in the biblical story and submitting to whatever you see there. Let *that* inform your commitments to one another. If you have been working through this book together, you have already done that. Now take the bold step of writing your commitments and marking this covenant with some kind of ritual or sign.

In Scripture there are two parts of a covenant—the *content* and the *sign*. The content includes (1) a clear articulation of the reality or the essence we are trying to live, preserve, protect and cultivate, and (2) the specific attitudes, behaviors and practices we are committed to that will help us live our intention in concrete ways. In the case of the Israelites, the reality God was inviting them to live into was their identity as people belonging to God—a treasured possession, a priestly kingdom (Ex 19:5-6). The covenant commitments that would preserve, protect and cultivate this reality were contained in the Ten Commandments and many other related instructions.

When the time came to ratify the covenant, Moses gathered the people and told them all the words the Lord had spoken, and the people responded verbally, "All the words that the LORD has spoken we will do" (Ex 24:3). Burnt offerings and the blood of the sacrifices were the signs of the covenant. A permanent and public recording of the covenant was made—first in the form of the stone tablets Moses brought down from the mountain and eventually in the Torah. In that way, the expectations about what it meant to be a part of this group under God were clear and always accessible. This is a compelling framework within which to consider our own covenant relationships.

It is important that we make our covenant very humbly and with a great deal of realism about our chances for actually being true to it. Some groups create very impressive documents by throwing just about every idealistic possibility they can think of on a piece of paper and calling it a covenant. I have seen the heartbreak and disillusionment that result when those very same leaders fail to abide by that covenant when the stakes seem too high.

One more thing to remember: we cannot force people to be who they don't want to be or to do what they don't want to do or are unable to do. Neither can we force them to do or be what they said they wanted to do or be before they fully understood what it would demand of them. This is very humbling. We would like to believe that we can control the outcome of things by casting vision, facilitating process, being clear, being loving or whatever. But leadership is not about control. All those who lead covenant communities will experience disappointment and disillusionment. Look what happened to Moses when he came down from the mountain! And he had a whole lot more to work with than many of us do—signs and wonders, a very cool staff, a cloud by day and pillar of fire by night, God's voice booming from the mountaintop—and yet the people reneged on the covenant.

Regardless of the initial enthusiasm, some people inevitably don't make it for the long haul and disappoint the group. And it hurts. There is no way around it. All we can do is keep inviting people to participate. We can cast vision. We can love the people God gives us to the best of our ability. We can do our best to clarify guiding values and principles, and to live them ourselves. We can try to call out the best in people when they falter. We can confess our own sins. But in the end the invitation to participate in such a community is from God. Ultimately, people don't answer to us, they answer to God. So do we. All we can control is our own response to the invitation to community and our own faithfulness to the covenant we have made to honor God and others.

WORKING THE PROCESS

The most important part of this chapter is the process you and your leadership group will undertake to translate all the work you have done and develop it into a written covenant to protect your life in community. The *content* of your covenant is the guiding values, principles and practices you have already articulated and agreed upon; the covenant captures these good intentions in writing and then provides a concrete action that gives each person the opportunity to make their commitment real.

In our own leadership community the process of establishing a covenant has gone something like this. There were a few values that some of us articulated in the first place, values that called us together and shaped our early identity—community gathered around the presence of Christ, spiritual transformation, solitude, silence and discernment, as described in chapter five. Then we identified practices that helped us live those values, and we practiced those from the first minute of our life together—fixed-hour prayer, following the lectionary, going on retreat regularly, practicing solitude and silence, finding ourselves in the story, discerning God's will together. This was our earliest attempt at developing a rule of life, but we had not yet captured it in writing or made an official covenant with each other.

Over the years, through our continued learning together and the school of hard knocks, we discovered additional values and practices, and added those to our rule of life as well. Eventually, we wrote down all our accumulated values and practices but soon realized that we needed to go beyond capturing what was happening in writing and move toward making a covenant by

1. clarifying our values with each other, noting key Scriptures God had used with us along the way

2. identifying the practices that help us to live those values in concrete ways

3. learning about and experimenting with a realistic and doable rhythm of practicing the disciplines

4. recording our values and practices, providing copies to the group, and inviting their input

5. incorporating that input and presenting it again for the group's final approval

6. ratifying (making real) the covenant through symbol and ritual at an annual leadership retreat

At a designated prayer service we signed duplicate documents so one could be kept on file in our offices and individuals could keep one for their personal reference. One of our members led us in a meditation reminding us of what it meant for us to covenant together. Then we each placed a stone on the altar as a sign and symbol of our commitment to this covenant, reminiscent of the twelve stones from the Jordan River the Israelites piled up as a memorial to what God had done for them (Josh 4:1-9). The stones were a symbol of our intent—that to the best of our ability we were covenanting to uphold and live out these values together and that each member was mutually responsible for holding the group accountable to the covenant.

Then we made sure that this "covenanting" service was not just a one-time occurrence. At our annual leadership retreat we review our covenant and talk about how we are doing with it. We discuss whether there is anything we need to add. We incorporate anyone new into the leadership community and discuss the covenant with them so they can join us when we renew our covenant with God and each other for another year. Recently, we developed a simple bookmark that includes our prayer of commitment and the covenant stipulations in an abbreviated form. We carry it with us as a sign of our covenant and as a reminder to keep praying for the health of our community.

Because community at the leadership level is so challenging, articulating covenant commitments and embracing them together in God's presence is of utmost importance. While we will continue to fine-tune our guiding values, principles and practices, it is essential for us to bind our hearts together around those values that are clear to us and that we can agree upon right now. We make this covenant for the sake of this community that is one expression of the body of Christ, for the integrity of the mission God has entrusted to us, and for the sake of Christ's kingdom. "Thy kingdom come, thy will be done, on earth as it is in heaven." Amen.

In Community

PRACTICING TOGETHER

Consider developing a covenant around your guiding values and the spiritual practices that will help you live your values. You do not need to get this done all in one session. (If you do try to do it in one session, make it a full meeting with no other agenda, or go on retreat for this specific purpose.) Although crafting a covenant is a group effort, it will help to have one person facilitate the process to make sure you keep moving. You might also designate a person to record in writing what the group has said so the facilitator is free to listen to and interact with the group. (Note: You may want to wait to finalize the covenant until after you have worked through the chapters on corporate discernment as there may be some things there you want to add.)

1. Capture in writing the guiding values and principles you wish to embrace together. List everything important to the group. Then make the list more manageable by grouping those things that fit together. (Hopefully, most of this work has already been done in conjunction with chapter six.)

2. Clarify which practices will help you to live each value. Some practices help you live more than one value (e.g., fixed-hour prayer provides a concrete way to open to the presence of Christ through prayer, Scripture reading, silence and worship). It may work best to agree on a value and then the practice that will help you live out that value. Then you can move on to discussing the next value.

   So for instance, you might agree that one of your values is to find ways to open to Christ's presence when you are together, and the practice you will engage in to help you live that value is praying at one or two of the fixed-hour prayer times, including time built in for silence and the reading of Scripture. Or you might agree to open your meeting with Scripture reading in the style of *lectio divina* and then share what you hear God saying to you. Or perhaps you decide to just open your meetings with a short period of silence to create space for individuals to listen to God as they begin. In other examples, you may agree that spiritual transformation is one of the values to which you are committed, so you could talk about what your commitment will be to a personal rule of life. If you value sane rhythms of work, rest and living within limits, that might lead you to make concrete decisions about Sabbath-keeping, regular solitude and vacation policies. Allow the Holy Spirit to guide your group in establishing your own unique rhythms/rule of life in community.

3. Decide on rhythms that are realistic for you: when and how often you will pray, read Scripture, go on retreat and so on. How will you structure your meetings to include the spiritual and relational practices that give ample opportunity for being open to God with each other? Be as specific as you can be at this time. (Some things can be figured out later through trial and error.)

4. After you have completed the rough draft of your values and practices, distribute to everyone in the group the record of what has been discussed, giving them time to reflect on whether there is anything missing or that needs to be corrected. They also need to agree that they are willing to commit to these values and practices. Make the changes on the master document and make copies so everyone has the final and complete version.

5. Decide together on a meaningful sign or ritual that would give you the opportunity to commit to the covenant as a group. Perhaps someone in your group has a particular gift for planning moments like this. If this is someone the group trusts, let them run with it so they can bless the group with their gifts in this area. It may be a great relief to the facilitator to have another member of the group lead the commitment ceremony. It doesn't

need to be anything fancy or overdone, but it should have some weight to it—something that members can point to as a reminder of the commitment they have made.

A PRAYER OF COMMITMENT

(If you choose to pray this together as part of your covenant-making process, the designated leader will read the words in lower case and everyone will read the words in small caps.)

As Abraham left his home
and the security of all he had known,

SO WE LAY DOWN WHAT IS PAST
AND LOOK TO THE FUTURE.[3]

As Elijah left his life in the company of others
to seek God in the wilderness,

SO WE COMMIT OURSELVES TO SEEK GOD
IN THE WILDERNESS OF OUR OWN SILENCE.

As Bartimaeus cried out to Jesus
and begged for mercy,

SO WE CAST OURSELVES ON GOD'S MERCY
FOR OUR OWN HEALING AND TRANSFORMATION.

As the Israelites travelled together in community
as the disciples gathered around the presence of Christ,

SO WE COMMIT OURSELVES TO GOD AND TO EACH OTHER
FOR THE JOURNEY OF SPIRITUAL TRANSFORMATION
AND DISCERNING GOD'S WILL TOGETHER
IN THIS COMMUNITY.

In the name of the Father, Son, and Holy Spirit.

THANKS BE TO GOD![4]

PART TWO

PRACTICING

DISCERNMENT

TOGETHER

GET READY

PREPARING FOR THE DISCERNMENT PROCESS

*The ongoing leadership of Christ in the world through
the Holy Spirit is described not simply as an incidental matter
in the Bible; it is presented as the pinnacle of Jesus' mission, continuing
throughout the history of the Church—his flock. The question,
therefore, is how to prepare ourselves to be in
a position to be led by Christ.*

PAUL ANDERSON

The staff and elders of Grace Church were excited that it was finally time to learn more about the spiritual discipline of *leadership* discernment and begin practicing it together. They had been faithful to the personal preparation of each individual leader; they had done the big work of cultivating the group as a community for discernment by establishing guiding values and transforming practices. The prayer service in which they had committed themselves to their covenant had been quite moving, and they knew they were on a whole different path as a group.

Elements of discernment were already showing up frequently in their planning meetings. Individuals felt free to reference a sense of consolation or desolation, and the group honored it. They could speak about something they heard from God in solitude and silence, and it was received with great respect. It was no longer unusual for someone to confess a false-self pattern that had affected the group, and the group was now able to extend compassion and forgiveness. When someone in the group sensed that a decision had been rushed or had been made primarily from human strategy rather than deep listening to God and each other, he or she could call attention to it and the group was willing to slow down and take more time for listening. They were becoming a community for discernment!

But they were also facing decisions of such significance that they were hesitant to make a commitment without a clear sense of God's will. They didn't yet know how to approach these larger decisions in a discerning way as a group, but they were certain these decisions required more than human wisdom and strategic thinking. By now they had learned that just because something makes sense on some level, that does not mean it is God's will. They were ready for the Holy Spirit to teach them those things that cannot be taught by human wisdom. They were painfully (or deliciously!) aware that they were completely dependent on God's promise to give wisdom to those who ask.

One of the biggest issues they faced was the growth the church was experiencing. As the staff and elders went through this very intimate experience of becoming a community for discernment, they recognized a new wind of the Spirit blowing through the congregation as well. Even though they had lost some members who were not ready for the rigors of the spiritual journey as it was now being presented in the church, other more serious spiritual seekers were finding their way in. They were strangely compelled by the depth and power of what was taking place in the lives of their leaders; although they would have been hard-pressed to describe this change in words, they knew that something was different, and it drew them to be a part of whatever it was that was happening.

The leadership group was committed to not doing anything that would derail them from continuing on the discernment-in-community track they were on. They knew they had to make good decisions about stewarding the growth that God was giving. The elders understood that it was their job to discern this (with input from the staff and congregation), but other teams were aware that they needed discernment as well. For a long time the children's ministry had been aware that providing an after-school program for at-risk children would meet a desperate need in their community and extend the positive impact they were having on the lives of kids they were ministering to. They weren't sure, however, whether God was really calling them to meet this need or if they could actually handle it. The senior pastor and the executive team had several new initiatives they were considering, and now they had the desire to go through the discernment process rather than just doing things that seemed like a good idea. They were ready to enter into a *practice* for seeking God's will together regarding these specific issues.

Personal Reflection

Earlier we noted that several New Testament stories illustrate leadership discernment in the early church. In Acts 6:1-7 there were minority complaints—widows who were being neglected in the daily distribution of food. Acts 15 records a disagreement about doctrine and practice—did Gentiles need to be circumcised in order to become Christ followers? In Acts 21:10-14 Paul was bent on going to Jerusalem, but a group of Christians in Caesarea thought he should not go because he would be taken captive. Take a few moments to read and reflect on these experiences of corporate discernment and notice elements of leadership discernment that you can glean from them.

GET READY, GET SET, GO!

There are three major phases in a good discernment process: get ready (the preparation phase), get set (gathering the community around the presence of Christ relative to the issue for discernment) and go (actual discernment)! Each phase of leadership discernment involves several moves; it is not, however, a mechanical process nor is it always linear. As we become more comfortable with the process we experience it not so much as a step-by-step procedure but as a creative mix of dynamic elements. Here are the basic moves.

Movements in Discernment

Get Ready: *Preparation*	• clarify the question for discernment • gather the community for discernment • affirm (or reaffirm) guiding values and principles
Get Set: *Putting Ourselves in* *a Position to Be Led*	• prayer for indifference • test for indifference • the prayer for wisdom • the prayer of quiet trust
Go: *Discerning God's* *Will Together*	• listen to what brought the question for discernment • listen to each other • listen to pertinent facts and information • listen to inner dynamics • silence—create space for God • reconvene and listen again • select and weigh the options • agree together • seek inner confirmation
Do: *The Will of God*	• communicate with those who need to know • make plans to do God's will as you have come to understand it

(For a downloadable version of this chart, see www.transforming center.org.)

GET READY

The first phase is all about *getting ready*—sort of like getting ready to paint a room. First we need to select the color, buy the paint, get the tools together, scrape off the peeling paint or strip the old wallpaper, lay out the paint brushes, put down drop cloths, do some taping and maybe do some priming. All of this is mere preparation. You're not actually painting yet and it can feel pretty tedious. *However,* if you know anything about painting, you know that these preliminary steps are essential for a good paint job.

We've all had the experience of taking shortcuts (we were in a hurry to get the job done) only to discover that the paint job did not turn out well because we scrimped on the preparation. The edges were sloppy because we didn't do a good job of taping. The paint covered unevenly because we didn't scrape or sand. We ran out of paint in the middle of the job because we didn't calculate carefully how much we would need. Paint got on the carpet or a piece of furniture because we didn't put down enough drop cloths. Through experience we learn that lack of preparation can be *disastrous* when it comes to painting—and leadership discernment! Following are the necessary preparations.

Clarify the question for discernment. Not all questions warrant a full discernment process. Some decisions, such as choosing a computer system or ordering new carpet for the sanctuary, can be made on the basis of a fifteen-minute, fact-filled discussion presented by a subcommittee appointed to do the research and make a proposal. However, other questions require a different level of attention and prayerfulness from the leadership, and it is good to have some agreement about what those areas are. Here are a few suggestions for determining what kinds of decisions warrant a full discernment process:

- Decisions that shape your identity and mission, policies, values and direction.

- Allocation of significant resources (money, time, human resources, organizational energy and focus). Allocation of resources reflects what we value. And in the end, it shapes who we
  become. For instance, choosing to allocate resources to build
  bigger and more expensive facilities communicates something
  of what we value. It also determines where a good portion of our
  energy and focus will be—at least for a period of time. "Where
  your treasure is, there will your heart be also," Scripture tells us.
  So decisions about money need to be carefully discerned because these reflect where the community's heart is and shape
  the community's priorities over time. Bigger is not necessarily
  bad, but bigger is also not necessarily better—especially if it
  taxes the community beyond its human and financial resources.
  Decisions to get bigger and do more will determine certain priorities and shape who we are, in the short term and in the long
  term.

  One very significant function of leadership is the stew-
  ardship of what some authors call "organizational energy." This
  is a less tangible resource than, say, money, but it is real and it
  is finite. Any decision that is a significant expenditure of organizational energy needs to be discerned well. Deciding where
  we are going to invest our treasure (money, human resources,
  time, energy and focus) needs to be discerned by spiritual
  people who are committed to spiritual discernment regarding
  such matters.

- *Key personnel* (staff, board members and high-level volunteers)
  who will have significant influence on direction and decision
  making, or who will represent the church or organization to
  others. Even the receptionist (the front-line person who represents your church or organization to the public), custodian
  (who is in the building at all hours of the day or night and has
  keys to everything), treasurer and bookkeeper (who handles

funds and keeps financial records) should be people whose character as well as skill has been discerned by spiritual people in the community.[1]

- Decisions affecting the *pace and quality of life for staff and constituency.* Decisions to add another church service or ministry initiative or to introduce a new innovation often get made in the ivory tower of upper-level leadership, even though those leaders may or may not have enough information to consider the impact it will have on those who must carry it out. While a certain idea might make sense strategically, seem like a necessity or be just plain cool, someone needs to ask questions about whether staff will still be able to observe a sabbath, what it will require of volunteers or whether it will push people to a point where their family lives or ability to maintain spiritual rhythms will be compromised. Part of spiritual leadership is asking these kinds of questions.

One of the most important aspects of my own discernment regarding key initiatives is conversations with administrative and operational associates seeking a realistic perspective on the impact of such decisions on our staff and volunteers, and on my own schedule—which they often see more clearly than I do. Talking about pace of life issues can be mighty clarifying! Since the work that God is doing *in* us is just as important as the work God is doing *through* us, decisions that have the potential to enhance or inhibit the work God is doing in us need to go through the discernment process.

It can greatly simplify matters for your leadership team if you can agree on some general guidelines about what kinds of issues and questions require discernment. This way, you don't have to wonder every time an issue comes up. However, there are times when something comes up that falls outside these categories and it is unclear whether special discernment is required. When this happens, simply check in with each other by asking, "Is this a matter for discernment?" If the group agrees that this is an area where wisdom from God is needed, then frame the question as clearly as possible and move into discernment with it.

The question beneath the question. Even when we think we know what the question is and have agreed that it is a matter for discernment, there might be a larger question lurking underneath that holds even greater significance for us. You will want to be alert to this possibility. The question about a new building project might deepen into a question about mission and values and whether a new building might or might not help us stay true to these. Does the mission we have had still hold true, and if so, is a new building consistent with it? Is God calling forth something new, or does our understanding of our mission and how it is to be carried out need to be nuanced?

What starts out as a meeting to set strategy gives way to the deeper question of whether we are pushing our own agenda or whether God is really opening up new opportunities. What begins as a question about event scheduling raises a more far-reaching concern about pace of life and whether we are working and living together in such a way that we honor human limitations and create space in our lives for loving God and others.

The preparation for discernment continues with listening for the real issue or question and then framing it as a question for discernment. Since Christ is the head of the church, the real question is, *What is the mind of Christ on this matter?* Discernment is never about what we think or prefer or are comfortable with. It is always about seeking the mind of Christ. If the presenting issue is that your church or organization is bursting at the seams, you probably have some idea of the options—build a bigger building, hive off and start something new in another location, or adopt a satellite strategy. But keep in mind that when we are entering into a discernment process, the question is not, What is the most strategic thing for us to do? or What do we *think* we should do? or What do the consultants recommend? The question for discernment is, *What is the mind of Christ* regarding how we are to respond to the church growth we are experiencing? Even the way we frame the question will affect how we proceed. So while it may seem obvious, the discernment process starts with making sure everyone agrees on what the real question is, and that it is a matter you are willing to discern together.

The process of discernment invites us into the heart and life of the Triune God. Decision-making can no longer be defined as doing what we think is best; it is now a search for the mind and will of God within a community of people with whom God has chosen to dwell.

DANNY MORRIS AND CHARLES OLSEN, *DISCERNING GOD'S WILL TOGETHER*

The need for discernment often arises because something is going on among us that warrants our attention, and we are willing to wonder together what it means and what God might be saying or doing through it. This is actually how the question for discernment got clarified in the New Testament church in Acts 15. Something new was happening among them—the Holy Spirit was being poured out among the Gentiles, and they were coming to faith in Christ. For the Jewish Christians this was unexpected since they had known themselves to be God's uniquely chosen people. Although this new development was a source of joy for Jewish believers, it did raise a question: Is it necessary for the Gentiles to be circumcised in order to be fully accepted into the community of faith? So, the need for discernment was sparked by two things— God was doing something new *and* there was significant disagreement about how to respond.

Up to that time, no one would have dared to question whether a man needed to be circumcised to become part of this new community. Circumcision was a sacred cow, and yet it was now up for debate because of something God was doing! Of course there would be differing opinions and even conflict! "No small dissension and debate," the Scriptures call it (Acts 15:2). So it was actually the presence of conflict (disagreement, debate, dissension) that clarified the question for discernment. Sometimes conflict is a signal that there is something to pay attention to, some new direction of the Spirit that needs to be discerned.

Gather the community for discernment. Once the issue for discernment has been clarified, we need to give careful thought to getting the right people involved. Of course there is *the identified leadership group*—those who are responsible, in the end, to discern the will of God and do it. Through some sort of congregational procedure, denominational appointment, board vote or hiring process, these are the ones God has appointed to bear the mantle of leadership in this particular sphere of influence. It is expected that these individuals are intentional about their ongoing transformation *and* that they are practicing discernment in their personal decision making.

Within this group a *leader* or *facilitator* of the discernment process needs to be identified if that is not clear. The facilitator could be the board (elder, committee) chair but not necessarily. Someone other than the chairperson might be more gifted and experienced at guiding a discernment process. Or the group might decide that they can utilize that leader's contribution more effectively if they bring someone in to facilitate.

In the Quaker tradition the person who presides at a meeting for discernment is called a clerk or a convener. Friends (or Quakers) regard meetings where leaders of the community come together to discern God's will as "a meeting for worship in which business is conducted." The clerk or presiding officer calls the meeting together as a meeting for worship, and begins with either prayer or a few minutes of silence or quiet worship. As matters are discussed and deliberations on important matters ensue, the Clerk will often introduce times of prayer or quiet waiting during the meeting as well. As members share about their deepening understanding of the issues, there may be the emergence of potential ways forward. The Clerk also will gather input from all sides of the issue, wanting to be sure that alternative perspectives are a direct part of the deliberations. Conducting the session as an intentional meeting for worship lifts our focus from the mundane to the divine. Therefore, the question is not "What is 'expedient'" or "What is the easiest route to take?" The goal is discerning Christ's will for the meeting, and we believe his will is not divided, but unitive.[2]

Another important function of the clerk is to gather the "sense of the meeting" (or a sense of how the Spirit is leading) and reflect that back to the group to see if it resonates as being true. This was at least part of James's function in Act 15:13-21, when he summed up all that had been said, related it to Scripture and then articulated his conclusion about what the Spirit was saying. In this case the apostles and the elders, with the consent of the whole church, were able to affirm James's "sense of the meeting," and they were able to move forward with the will of God as it had been made clear to them.

In their book, *Discerning God's Will Together,* Danny Morris and Chuck Olsen have coined the term *discernmentarian* to designate the chosen guide for a discernment process who eventually signals the outcome of the meeting. Just as a parliamentarian (someone who understands and can guide parliamentary procedures) is commonly called on to give leadership in the process of majority rule, a spiritual guide experienced with the movements of spiritual discernment can provide leadership in a discernment process.

If the group chooses to recognize a discernmentarian, that person should be someone the group trusts and who has enough experience in the role (here or in other groups) to be able to help the group move forward. He or she should be gifted in the area of discernment, sensitive and spiritually attuned to what's going on in the group, able to identify and call out the spiritual gifts of others during the group process. This should be a person the group recognizes as being fair and able to maintain objectivity and a prayerful stance. This person exhibits patience and has the ability to see a process through to a good end without rushing. This person needs to be accepted and trusted by everyone in the group.

If the group's regular chairperson has the character and training of a discernmentarian, and the group trusts him or her in that role, it is fine for one person to assume both the role of chairperson *and* discernmentarian. If not, the group may need to consider bringing in a discernmentarian from outside the group who can facilitate and hold a good process in place.[3]

In the Transforming Center, I have always led the discernment process because that is my area of expertise and training. However, there are times when, as founder of the organization, I think it would be better if someone else facilitated the discernment process so I could be more involved in the listening and discussion without having the burden of facilitation. Sometimes when it seems best for me to participate more fully rather than facilitate, I have asked someone else to lead portions of the discernment process so I can listen, be a prayerful presence and offer my own perspective without having to hold the whole process in place for everyone.

The question of who will lead the discernment process is important for the group and could significantly affect whether discernment is what actually takes place. Whatever you call this person and whether they are from within or outside the group, the leader of such a process needs to be a differentiated, nonanxious presence (to use the language of family systems theory). He or she needs to have the capacity to die to self and relinquish control when appropriate, and be aware of his or her own growing edges of energy, passion and limitations. This person should not see him- or herself as wiser than the group but calling out the wisdom of the group. The leader is able to hold a safe space in which the group can interact productively, and he or she needs to understand corporate discernment well enough to help the group know where they are in the process so they can keep moving. Above all, the leader needs to help the group remain focused on seeking the mind of Christ.

Another category of involvement that Morris and Olsen helpfully identify is the role of *sage*. This is a person of wisdom and experience who is respected by the group because he or she possesses practical insight won through life experience and longevity in the community.

> In Israel's ancient days, sages were called elders. They were shrewd observers of life; they knew what produced happiness, prosperity, justice and peace. They sat at the gates of the village in order to make their wisdom available to the whole community. A body of wisdom literature grew out of their insights.[4]

A sage does not necessarily need to have a vote (if that's what your polity requires in order to ratify a decision) but can be invited to contribute wisdom to the process. The sage's gifts and contributions should be affirmed in such a way that the group truly does benefit from the wisdom he or she has to offer. And depending on the issue at hand, there could be a different sage involved at different times, depending on availability or the areas of experience and expertise in the area being discerned.

Another important function in a group gathered for discernment is that of an *intercessor*—someone gifted and called to hold the group in prayer as they proceed. The intercessor is present to God on behalf of the individual or the group—like Moses was present to God on behalf of the Israelites during the battle with the Amalekites in Exodus 17. In this case the battle was won and lost on the basis of Moses' ability to remain faithful in intercessory prayer. An intercessor may be visibly present in the room, in which case he or she does not generally participate in the discussion or debate. Alternatively, the intercessor may be praying off site but is aware that the group is meeting and discerning important matters. He or she might even have a copy of the agenda to pray along with the group throughout the allotted meeting time.

For a long time we did not have an intercessor in the Transforming Center. Such a person had not yet been given to us, and we experienced it as a real lack in our community life. *We longed for God to give us an intercessor.* Finally, God did give us this gift—someone who had come through the Transforming Community experience and grew into the role in a gradual and graced way. While the presence of a gifted intercessor does not diminish the responsibility the rest of us have to pray and intercede, it has been amazing to have someone officially recognized in this role—a praying presence for the ministry as a whole who is present with us in a more focused way during important moments when we need the wisdom and guidance of the Holy Spirit. It is never assumed that she will speak up in our meetings, and it is not her desire to do so. However, we often ask her if there is anything that has come to her in her praying. At times she has sensed something from God, which we receive. Hers is a presence and a voice we have come to trust.

The intercessor's role is very sensitive and requires a great deal of humility and trust among all the individuals involved. It is good to let it develop gradually to the comfort of all.

You will also need to identify a *scribe* or *secretary* to keep a record of what takes place—particularly who was present in the meeting, any agreements that were reached and a general summary of how that agreement was reached. It is good to have this written documentation for accuracy and to confirm agreements. It is inspiring to have a record of how God has been active among us through the work of the Holy Spirit.

Who else do we need? Once the basic group has been identified and roles have been clarified, you might ask whether anyone else needs to be involved or any other voices need to be heard. Is there anyone else who has gifts of wisdom and discernment, information and expertise that could be valuable relative to this issue? Are there any other influencers who might be able to help communicate the outcomes of our process to others in the larger community when the time comes?

It is amazing how we can become so stuck in organizational silos that we overlook those who might have important contributions to make just because they are outside our normal purview. So, in addition to the individuals who make up the leadership group, there might be other voices the group needs to hear in order to make a fully informed decision. Such voices might include:

- those who will be affected by the decision (such as the converted Gentiles in Acts 15)

- those who have experiences that are pertinent to the issue being considered (Peter, Paul and Barnabas, who had witnessed these conversions)

- those who have special expertise or have done research in the area being considered, or those who have special anointing and calling regarding the issue being discussed (like Peter, who had been anointed by God to bring the gospel to the Gentiles)

- those who have to carry out the course of action that we decide on (key staff or volunteers, administrative or operations personnel, etc.)

All of these have special wisdom to offer. It is not assumed that all these voices will be present for the whole process or that they will have an official vote, but they are voices that need to be heard. Our decisions will be wiser and more realistic if we invite them to speak and we listen to what they have to say. Ask God to guide you in the process of identifying which voices need to be heard for there to be a complete perspective.

Affirm (or reaffirm) guiding values and principles. Entering a discernment process with other leaders requires clarity about what values govern the process and create a safe environment. Though you have already established guiding values and principles for your life together in community, the beginning of a new discernment process is a good time to reaffirm your commitment to those values and principles, especially in the midst of the rigorous discussion, debate and differing points of view. If you have a sense that there might be disagreement or difficult conversations ahead, it is good to be reminded of the values you will not violate for any reason. At the beginning of a discernment process, you might want to reiterate your commitment to seek God's will and to be trustworthy in how you relate to each other.

Many aspects of God's will are already clear to us: we are to love one another, to seek unity with one another, tell each other the truth, value each other's gifts and contributions, be kind and treat others with honor and respect, confess our sins and go to one another directly when we are hurt and offended so we can regain fellowship. If, in a discernment process, we come to a decision on an important issue but have disregarded the mind and heart of Christ regarding how we treat one another, have we truly discerned the will of God? On any day, before we ask for further revelation, our commitment is to the basic will of God as it has already been revealed. Given the divisions and factions we see in churches and Christian organizations today, this aspect of the will of God cannot be emphasized enough.

One of the great contributions of the Quaker tradition on the topic of corporate discernment is that unity is a fundamental marker that God's will has been discerned. Quaker author Eden Grace puts it this way, "Since Christ is not divided, the nearer we come to him, the nearer we will be to one another. Thus the sense of being led into Unity with one another becomes a fundamental mark of the Divine work in the world."[5] As part of your preliminary work in getting ready for discernment, you might want to discuss the importance of unity in discerning the mind of Christ. How far are we willing to go without that unity? What will it mean to us if we don't reach consensus, and what will we do at that point? (This will be discussed more fully in chapter eleven.)

In addition to guiding values and principles there might be parameters specific to the issue you are dealing with. If so, it's good to make that clear at the outset so everyone is in agreement. For instance, when Transforming Center leaders are seeking discernment about new board members or ministry leaders, we have one very important guiding principle: potential leaders in the organization have to have completed (or be in the process of completing) a Transforming Community experience. This experience is our board orientation process, our staff and novitiate training, and our community covenant all rolled into one. Our ministry is founded on shared values and practices in community; we want to go forward with those who are in unity with us around these things. There can be carefully considered exceptions to this principle, but we are very cautious about it. Nearly every time we have violated this principle, even if we thought we had good reason, we have regretted it. This narrows the field of potential leaders in a very helpful way.

Once a painter has chosen the paint, laid out the brushes, taped the edges and covered the furniture, he or she is ready to paint. Once your leadership group has clarified the question for discernment, gathered the right people as the community for discernment, and affirmed (or reaffirmed) guiding values and principles, you are ready to cross the threshold into the actual process of discernment.

In Community

PRACTICING TOGETHER

1. Take time to allow different members of the group to share what they learned about leadership discernment in the passages referenced at the beginning of this chapter: Acts 6:1-7; 15:1-21; 21:10-14. (If you are very brave, go on to Acts 15:36-41.) How do these passages impact your group as you prepare to discern?

2. How do you respond to the Quaker idea of the leadership meeting as "a meeting for worship in which business is conducted"?

3. If you have an issue or a question for discernment, prepare for the discernment process by working through the moves in this chapter and applying them to the issue at hand: clarify the question for discernment, identify the people who need to be involved and decide how you will include them, and affirm (or reaffirm) guiding values and principles, including any specific parameters that apply specifically to what you are discerning.

CLOSING PRAYER
O God, by whom we are guided in judgment,
and who raises up for us light in the darkness,
Grant us, in all our doubts and uncertainties,
the grace to ask what you would have us to do;
That your spirit of wisdom
may save us from all false choices,
and in your straight path we may not stumble;
through Jesus Christ our Lord.
Amen.[6]

GET SET

FROM DECISION MAKING TO DISCERNMENT

God's will, nothing more, nothing less, nothing else.

DANNY MORRIS AND CHARLES OLSEN

❧

The Grace Church leadership group embraced the preparatory phase. They could see how such preparations were necessary and that, over time, it would take less time to get ready because their values and practices would already be in place. Now they were ready to learn about the actual practice of discernment.

SETTLING IN

When a group gathers for discernment, it can be helpful to do something that helps participants "get set" or put themselves in a position to be led—both as individuals and as a group. This helps them "cross the threshold" from where they are into a sharper awareness of their identity as a community gathered to discern the will of God.

Settling in to community could involve a short service of fixed-hour prayer, a brief time of worship, a guided meditation followed by time spent in silence, *lectio divina* or a time of checking in with each other using a meaningful question such as, What are you leaving behind in order to be here, and to what will you be returning? or Where are you experiencing consolation (God's presence) or desolation (emptiness) in your life right now?

> Members of a Christian community who are seeking to find God in all things will be able to grow in intimacy by sharing their stories of what has happened to them as they have walked with Jesus in prayer, and how they have recognized him in their own lives. . . . Such an experience of intimacy in a community is unifying and energizing. It is an experience of the presence of Christ.[1]

After such sharing, there can be a brief silence in which individuals are invited to let go and trust God with whatever they are carrying. In this silence, group members should be encouraged to open themselves to receive the gift of God's presence as they enter the meeting's agenda.

THE PRAYER FOR INDIFFERENCE

After settling in, the group is ready to cross the threshold into discernment, and the prayer for indifference or freedom from inordinate attachment carries us across that threshold. In this prayer we ask God to make us indifferent to anything but the will of God relative to the matter we are gathered to discern. At the beginning of any leadership discernment process, it is good to be reminded to ask for the grace to be indifferent to matters of ego, prestige, organizational politics, personal opinion, personal advantage, personal preference or even ownership of a pet project. We ask God for the grace to desire his will—nothing more, nothing less, nothing else.

Praying for indifference may be the most counterintuitive move in the leadership discernment process. Many define leadership as having a compelling vision, a clear rationale and the ability to influence others. While these are important aspects of leadership—especially if the vision is God-given and there is an anointing by God to lead toward that vision—spiritual leadership is not fundamentally about *our* leadership. It is about putting ourselves and guiding the group into a position to be *led by Christ*, who is the true head of the church. Indifference is as crucial in leadership discernment as it is in personal discernment, which is why it is important for individuals to have had some experience with indifference in matters of personal discernment before trying to do it in a leadership setting.

There is a nuanced difference between the prayer *for* indifference and the prayer *of* indifference: in the prayer *for* indifference we humbly ask God for something that we do not yet have. The prayer *of* indifference comes *after* we have prayed the prayer *for* indifference and God has answered our prayer. Some writers call this gift "holy indifference" because it is brought about through the work of the Spirit and is given for the holy purpose of being open to a new work of God.

For most of us, coming to a place of indifference takes time, especially if we have a strong opinion about the matter at hand, it is something we are invested in, or it will affect us directly. Danny Morris and Chuck Olsen also use the term *shedding* to refer to the process of indifference and point out that

> the questions a person answers in the process of indifference are these: What am I willing to let die to give God room to start something new? What will I lay aside or leave behind so that I will be open to new gifts of grace or new expressions of ministry? People involved in the process of shedding may [need to] humble themselves or give up values they usually cherish in pursuit of the greater good. The process may mean spiritual death and resurrection.[2]

Obviously, each person will need to do their own spiritual work around the question of whether they are indifferent to anything but the will of God. Each will need to wrestle with this question in the context of his or her own intimacy with God and allow God to do God's work just as Jesus did in the garden of Gethsemane. His prayer—"Not my will but yours be done"—is another example of the prayer *of* indifference, and he was able to pray this only after a fierce spiritual struggle. In Jesus' struggle, the Scriptures describe him as being grieved and agitated to the extent that he threw himself down on the ground and prayed more than once "if it is possible, let this cup pass from me" (Mt 26:39).

The fact that Jesus expressed a strong desire to do things a different way indicates there is nothing wrong with having a preference, an opinion or a strong desire. But Jesus' struggle acknowledges the fact that there could be—and often is—a difference between our own preferences and the will of God. The fact that he asked more than once that this cup pass from him tells us that indifference doesn't always come easily or the first time we ask. His struggle *for* indifference resulted in a prayer *of* indifference that bore an uncanny resemblance to his mother's prayer thirty-three years earlier. This was not a superficial platitude merely meant to sound spiritual to whoever was listening. It was the hard-won prayer of indifference that would carry him across the threshold to discerning and doing the will of God.

THE TEST FOR INDIFFERENCE

Although the prayer for indifference is a deeply personal matter, its reality (or the lack thereof) in each person's life affects the group deeply. Once the question for discernment is clarified, experienced discerners will immediately start praying for indifference! But it is important to have a mechanism built in to the group's discernment process that helps individuals be honest about whether they are indifferent to anything but the will of God.

In the Quaker tradition this is called the *test for indifference*, in which the discernmentarian or the person leading the process asks, "How many are indifferent?" The members can then share their answer to this question. Some might be able to report that, by God's grace, they have come to the point of indifference. Others might say that they are attached to an outcome but are still praying about it, asking God to bring them to a place of indifference. Another might acknowledge a personal preference but report that he or she is able to hold that with open hands for the good of the group—or not, if that is the case. Obviously, the practice of self-examination over time fosters the kind of self-awareness that makes this kind of disclosure possible.

As challenging as attending to the question of indifference may be, it is time and energy well spent. If we do not reach the point of indifference, or if we are not at least honest about the fact that we are not indifferent, the discernment process becomes little more than a rigged election. In the leadership setting the process can deteriorate to nothing more than a tug of war between differing human agendas. The process of sharing our inner state with others can help loosen our grip on our own agenda and open ourselves to the wisdom of the group. If we are able to confess to the group that we are not indifferent, it can then become a part of the group's ongoing prayer and consideration of one another as we move through the rest of the process.

We need to make allowances for varying levels of indifference and of comfort when talking about such things. This is an opportunity for us to bear with one another as Christ bears with us. It takes a great deal of trust to talk about inner dynamics, which we are accustomed to dealing with very personally—if we are aware of them at all. Not all groups are trustworthy enough to do this. This is one of the reasons why cultivating community at the leadership level is so important; it provides an environment of trust within which these deeper dynamics of the soul can be shared.

And hopefully our souls are being shaped by God's grace working in and through the group.

Since indifference is something *God does in us* rather than something we can make happen, we enter into these proceedings openly and honestly before God, trusting God to do what needs to be done in our hearts. It can happen in a flash, even during the process. Something shifts inexplicably, and when it does, we know that God did it. It is no small thing. Quaker missionary and educator Thomas Kelly, in his classic work *A Testament of Devotion*, describes indifference as coming to the place where

> nothing else in all of heaven or earth counts so much as His will, His slightest wish, His faintest breathing. And holy obedience sets in, sensitive as a shadow, obedient as a shadow, selfless as a shadow. Not reluctantly but with ardor one longs to follow him the second half. Gladly, urgently, promptly one leaps to do His bidding, ready to run and not be weary and to walk and not faint.[3]

When a room full of leaders has prayed for indifference and God has done that work in their lives, they are in position to be led by the resurrected Christ through the real presence of the Holy Spirit. In this way we are seeking unity of spirit (the spirit of indifference to anything but the will of God) even when we don't have complete unity of mind. When the discernmentarian senses that everyone has been heard, he or she can summarize the group's situation by saying something like, "I sense that, by God's grace, we are indifferent on this matter. Thanks be to God!" Or "Some of us have reached a point where we are indifferent to anything but the will of God, and some of us are still praying for it. We thank you for your honesty. Let's keep praying for each other as we take the next step."

If this conversation has taken place honestly, we do not necessarily need to wait until everyone can indicate indifference. It is enough to have everyone's "stuff" on the table. However, the group may also feel that there hasn't been enough movement toward indifference on the part of enough individuals for discernment to be effective. In this case, and depending on the schedule, the discernmentarian could give time for silence or wait to proceed until the next meeting so adequate time and space is given for God to work. If, by chance, you are on retreat (which we often are when we are making big decisions), you can wait to continue until the next morning to give God space to work.

Personal Reflection

Bring to mind a question for discernment that your leadership group is facing; then take the test for indifference right now in the privacy of your own heart. Are you indifferent to anything but the will of God? Ask God to search your heart and give you self-knowledge about where you might be attached to anything other than God's will. If you are indifferent, thanks be to God. If not, don't judge yourself; just notice it with compassion. If you are willing to do so, ask, What needs to die in me in order for the will of God to find room in my life? What do I need to let go of in order to receive some new gift of God?

THE PRAYER FOR WISDOM

When we have reached a point of indifference or we have at least been honest with each other in acknowledging where we are in the process, we are finally ready to pray for wisdom. One of the great promises of Scripture is "If any of you is lacking in wisdom, ask God, who gives to all generously and ungrudgingly, and it will be given you" (Jas 1:5). This is a very humbling prayer for leaders—especially the point leader—because the prayer acknowledges that we are lacking in something, and we don't make that admission easily. It is one thing to admit our lack of wisdom to God in private, but when we are leading the group or leading the meeting, it is much harder to lead without having the answer or at least an opinion about the general direction we should go.

Second, the verse suggests that there is something important about actually asking God—in more than just a perfunctory and generalized way—for the wisdom we need. Many of us have been taught that leadership is having the answer, and we come into meetings we are leading prepared to bestow that wisdom on our trusty followers; we might ask God for wisdom in a prayer that sounds very spiritual, but the truth is, there isn't much room for God to do or say anything other than what we already have in mind. The prayer for wisdom needs to indicate that we are truly open to the wisdom of God, which is often foolishness to the thinking of the world. It may not fit with the wisdom found in the current *New York Times* bestseller list or the latest *Harvard Business Review* article on leadership.

This is why indifference *precedes* the prayer for wisdom. We need to be indifferent to our ego's need to be seen as wise by human standards. We need to be aware of and utterly detached from the false self's need for control, success and approval, or whatever else it longs for. Indifference prepares us to pray the prayer for wisdom *and* to receive it when it is given. So, an important part of the discernment process is to create space for waiting upon God and asking God for the wisdom we need relative to the issue that we're facing. This could be prayer with words, but eventually words fail. The deepest matters of the heart often transcend words, and, depending on the magnitude of what we are dealing with, the same is true of our need for wisdom.

I remember a time when our leadership community met to discuss our need for funding in order to stay in existence. We wondered together *what God was saying* through the fact that we couldn't seem to get funded at a level that would sustain us, let alone allow us to move forward. As we had our initial discussion and got all the issues on the table, the real question was clarified:

Should we go on, or should we just let go and shut it down? It was a terrible question but we knew we needed to ask it. And we had struggled with our financial realities enough that we had finally reached a place of indifference—both individually and as a group. This was very painful for some of us—especially me—but we really did not know what to do. We knew that the answer was beyond our ability to think it through. Our need for wisdom was profound and real; we were completely at the end of ourselves.

We were sitting around a large conference table when all of the pieces fell into place—the question for discernment was clear, each person was indifferent to anything but the will of God, and our need for wisdom was profound. At that point, without anyone saying anything, we all sank to the floor and knelt at our chairs. The reason I remember it so clearly is that it was so odd. Most of the time when people sit at big tables in a board room, they try to maintain some semblance of dignity! But there was none of that on this day as we all fell to our knees.

At first there were no words, just our bodies and spirits praying "with sighs too deep for words." It actually felt good to stop working so hard with our intellects and to trust Someone wiser than ourselves. The silence was weighty with longing, need and true poverty of spirit. Eventually there were some words that expressed our need and several prayed out loud, asking God for wisdom. And then more silence. After a time, someone closed that time of beseeching God for wisdom with a prayer that gathered everything up to God. We climbed back into our chairs and started to listen from an entirely different perspective.

I don't recall a lot of what happened after that but I do remember that someone put forth a "third way" that resonated as being true for the group. What I recall most clearly is how it felt to wait on God with these other leaders and to ask for wisdom in such a vulnerable and open way. I was grateful beyond words for the opportunity to, along with others, lead from this kind of dependency on

God rather than always pushing and striving for human answers. And we're still here, all these years later, doing fruitful ministry— so the wisdom that is from God clearly prevailed!

Sometimes discernment is like that; it comes from so far beyond ourselves that we experience it as a pure gift. We don't know how it happened, where it came from or if we deserve it; we just know it came, and we receive it as we receive all God's gifts—with gratitude and wonderment.

> ### Personal Reflection
> Take time to sit with your own longing and desire for wisdom relative to the issue your group is facing. As you feel ready, pray the prayer for wisdom in words that come from your own heart.

THE PRAYER OF QUIET TRUST

Another aspect of "getting set"—or getting ourselves into a position to be led by Christ—is the *prayer of quiet trust*, like the one found in Psalm 131.

O LORD, my heart is not lifted up,
    my eyes are not raised too high;
I do not occupy myself with things
    too great and too marvelous for me.
But I have calmed and quieted my soul,
    like a weaned child with its mother;
    my soul is like the weaned child that is with me.

In this prayer, the psalmist acknowledges his utter dependence on God in the face of matters "too great and too marvelous for me"—which actually means things that are too complicated and far beyond our ability to figure out. This was the silent prayer we fell into quite naturally in the experience I just described.

When we enter into the discernment process, we have already

acknowledged that the matter before us is beyond our ability to figure out through human effort alone. So this prayer is perfect! It gives us a way to rest in God and God's promises, and to experience that childlike trust that is so crucial to the journey of faith. "Whoever does not receive the kingdom of God as a little child," Jesus says, "will never enter it" (Mk 10:15). And the kingdom of God is, by definition, the state of being in which God reigns in our life and his presence is shaping our reality. The kingdom of God is here now, if we get ready and get set to receive it. And the way we get set is to become like a child, a very young child who recently has been weaned and is calmed and quieted just by being near his or her mother—the one whom the baby trusts utterly.

What an amazing picture of our relationship with God and the stance we can cultivate as we enter into discernment! But this is not the way we usually approach the leadership setting. Usually we come with our polished, powerful and in-control selves. But what if we created space for each of us to drop into that place of deep trust in God where we know and experience utter dependence on God—like a small child dependent on his or her parents for life and sustenance? The prayer of quiet trust creates that space and helps us make that shift.

In case you are concerned that all of this will take too much time and there are too many steps, this prayer does not have to be its own distinct step. In the prayer time I described earlier, the second time of silence—the one that came after our spoken prayers for wisdom—was actually the prayer of quiet trust. This prayer is usually silent because we are *experiencing* our utter dependence on God and resting in our deep trust of God. This does not require words. So when you have asked God for wisdom, fall silent as a group and experience the prayer of quiet trust. Cast yourselves upon God for what you need, and experience again how much you need God and how completely trustworthy God is. In the silence, we can touch and rest in that place deep inside where we know we can trust God's goodness.

A different kind of spirit descends on us when we make decisions from this stance. Once we have learned and practiced it, we can return to this prayer as often as we need to during the discernment process. When we sense that things are getting out of hand, that human dynamics are distracting us from real issues, that we are stuck, that we are applying nothing more than human effort, the leader can call the group back to this prayer of quiet trust and silence. This gives us the opportunity to shift back into a position of trust rather than human striving.

Personal Reflection

After you have prayed for wisdom, give yourself a few moments to sit quietly in God's presence, allowing the chaos of all human effort to settle down. Imagine yourself as a child, calmed and quieted by the presence of a loving parent. (If you did not have a parent that felt like a loving presence, imagine yourself on your best day as a loving parent [or aunt or uncle] and what it would be like to be quiet in that presence.) Drop down into that place where you are willing to trust God with everything that concerns you, knowing that the will of God is the best thing that can happen to you under any circumstances. Experience what it is like to be in that quiet, trusting stance. Imagine bringing yourself in that stance to your next leadership meeting.

PRAY WITHOUT CEASING

Prayer is an essential element in the discernment process, not only because prayer moves the heart of God but also because there are ways of praying that can produce profound shifts in us—shifts that help us to "get set" to receive what we are asking for. Obviously, these practices are much more than the perfunctory prayers that merely bookend our meetings and are perceived as being unrelated to the business at hand. In fact, it involves several kinds of praying that undergird the entire process, woven in and out like a bright thread woven throughout a beautiful piece of cloth. Pretty soon, without even being aware of it, we are praying without ceasing. And that changes everything.

The first objective is to bring apprentices to the point where they dearly love and constantly delight in the "heavenly father" made real to earth in Jesus and are quite certain that there is no "catch," no limit, to the goodness of his intention or to his power to carry them out.

DALLAS WILLARD, *THE DIVINE CONSPIRACY*

In Community

PRACTICING TOGETHER

Assuming that you have clarified the question for discernment, involved the right people and established guiding values and principles, proceed through the moves in this chapter relative to an issue you are discerning:

1. What is your response to the prayer for indifference? Are you willing to do the test for indifference as a group? Allow the leader or discernmentarian to lead you through this process.

2. After listening to each individual's response to the test for indifference, and after the leader/discernmentarian has brought closure to it, enter into the prayer for wisdom. Kneel if you would like to. If everyone agrees, change your location or your sitting configuration. Let it be understood that you will begin with a few moments of silence and then invite people to pray with words as

they are led. These prayers should be short, simple and even childlike. Individuals may pray more than once as they are led.

3. When the needed words have been said to God and the group seems ready to return to silence, the designated leader can read Psalm 131 and then allow the group to settle into the prayer of quiet trust for two to three minutes.

4. The leader can close the prayer time by using the following Scripture and prayer of response. The italicized words are read by all.

CLOSING PRAYER

A Reading from Scripture

For thus says the Lord GOD, the Holy One of Israel:

In returning and rest you shall be saved;
in quietness and confidence shall be your strength. . . .

Therefore the LORD waits to be gracious to you;
therefore he will rise up to show mercy to you.

For the LORD is a God of justice;
blessed are all those who wait for him.

(Is 30:15, 18)

Response

Oh God of peace,
who has taught us that in returning and rest
we shall be saved,
in quietness and confidence shall be our strength;

By the power of your Spirit open us, we pray,
to your presence,
where we may be still, and know that you are God,
through Jesus Christ our Lord.
Amen.[4]

11

Go!

DISCERNING AND DOING
GOD'S WILL TOGETHER

Christians at their best are good listeners,
and the Christian church, when most faithful,
is a listening community.

BISHOP RUEBEN JOB

❧

Ａs the leaders of Grace Church listened to the teaching on getting set and getting ready, they were beginning to see that discernment in community at the leadership level really is very different from decision making. They were a little concerned that such a process would take longer than what they were accustomed to and couldn't quite see how it would work in the press of their ministry lives. However, even though their minds were resistant, their hearts were deeply stirred by the prayer practices described in the "get set" stage of the discernment process.

At the end of the session in which their facilitator had described this part of the process, she led them in experiencing the prayer practices they had been learning. They put their papers and notes away, joined a circle and settled into a quiet, prayerful stance. A single candle was lit as a way of signifying Christ's presence with them through the Holy Spirit. Each individual brought to mind a real issue or question they were facing in their leadership—an area in which they knew they needed God's guidance—and held it openly in Christ's presence. Then the facilitator led them through a guided experience in the prayer for indifference and doing the test for indifference—interiorly this time since the group was a combination of several teams discerning different issues.

After a few minutes to consider the prayer for indifference and actually pray it, they were invited to pray simple, one-sentence prayers aloud—either praying for indifference (for those who didn't have it yet) or for wisdom (for those ready to receive it). They did not name the issue they were seeking to discern; they just named their desire to be made indifferent or to receive wisdom. It was a tender time of being together in God's presence.

When those who chose to offer a spoken prayer had done so, the facilitator read Psalm 131 and asked the group to sit for a few minutes in wordless prayer, waiting on God in quiet trust relative to the issues each had identified in the privacy of his or her own heart. The silence was full, it was restful, and it helped them to be more deeply grounded in the presence of God. When they debriefed the experience together, they were amazed at the shift that had taken place in their hearts—the letting go of ego-drivenness, the awareness of their own attachments, the willingness to trust God more fully with outcomes—and they knew, beyond a shadow of a doubt, that if they entered into discernment with each other from that spiritual stance, the outcomes would be qualitatively different. They were sold!

THE HEART OF THE MATTER

The heart of the discernment process is listening—to God, to each other and to what's going on in the depths of our own souls, where

God's Spirit witnesses with our spirit about things that are true. First, we listen deeply to whatever has brought this issue or question to the fore—whatever experience is causing us to be asking this question in the first place.

When the New Testament believers clarified their question for discernment in Acts 15—do Gentiles need to be circumcised in order to be saved?—things were happening among them that required them to rethink some of their basic assumptions, and they needed to respond with clear leadership. They were wise enough to know that it was significant enough that they couldn't rely on their knee-jerk reaction ("Of course they need to be circumcised! That's what has always been required!") or their ability to think it through strategically ("Well, let's see . . . if we make the membership requirements a little less strenuous, maybe more people will join the church!"). No, *they wanted to understand what God was up to.*

So they entered a time of listening: to the conversion experience of the Gentiles themselves; to in-person accounts from respected believers who had witnessed these conversions; to the perspectives of the Pharisees who were experts in Mosaic law; to Peter's perspective, which had been shaped by his special anointing to bring the gospel to the Gentiles; and to Paul and Barnabas's descriptions of signs and wonders God had done through them among the Gentiles. The whole assembly listened to all of this in silence (which in Jewish culture was a sign of respect) and with rapt attention.

Finally, in response to all he had heard, James expounded on Scripture, making the connection between the current phenomenon and the words of the Old Testament prophets. He connected the dots between Peter's testimony and the words of the prophet Amos, who described the trajectory of God's long-term plan: "And I will set it up, so that all other peoples may seek the Lord—even all the Gentiles over whom my name has been called" (Acts 15:17).

What James did was brilliant, from a spiritual perspective: he helped them see their own story within the larger story of God's redemptive purposes in the world, enabling them to understand what was going on *from that perspective*. Then he dared to state what he felt God was saying in it all: that the Gentiles did not need to become Jews (symbolized by the ritual of circumcision) but they did need to become God-worshipers, abstaining from immorality and from activities associated with idol worship.

James seemed to embody the roles we identified earlier—clerk, discernmentarian and sage. He was very experienced in the life of the community, was respected by the community for his wisdom and insight, and had a grasp of the overarching themes of Scripture. He may have even functioned as the leader or the discernmentarian—the one giving structure and guidance to the process; we don't know. The point is that the listening process had been so thorough and so disciplined for the purpose of discernment that James was able to gather it up and reflect meaning back to the group. When he did so, it was clear to everyone that the wisdom of God had been given. James's summary enabled the group to affirm a shared sense of how the Spirit was moving among them.

This story illustrates the fact that leadership discernment involves *a major commitment to listening* with love and attention (1) to the movement of the Holy Spirit in the world, (2) to the promptings of the Holy Spirit deep within ourselves and the group, (3) to Scripture, religious tradition (although sometimes it is the tradition that is being challenged, as it was in this case), pertinent facts and information, and the voices of those who will be affected by our decisions, *and* (4) to that place in us where God's Spirit witnesses with our spirit about those things that are true. The prayer practices we explored in chapter ten help us listen to God within. Now let's turn our attention to listening to God together. It begins with setting the agenda.

SET THE AGENDA

One of the most important roles for leaders is often hidden: praying through and setting the agenda for leadership meetings. When discernment is the goal, the agenda needs to be set and prepared for in such a way that the right information is available to the group before and during the meeting. The leader or facilitator needs to make sure the necessary voices are heard and that there is plenty of space for prayer, listening, silence and response. Over the years, I have discovered that preparing an agenda that flows well with the needed information and making sure the components of a discernment process are in place requires as much prayer and careful thought as anything else I do.

We could wish for a few more details regarding how the Jerusalem Council's discernment process was structured and who held the structure in place. It seems clear that there was a structure that someone had thought through because the meeting was carried out decently and in order for the purpose of listening to God. Nothing about that meeting seems random or haphazard, and the desired outcome was certainly accomplished—they were able to discern God's will together. There was someone (maybe James) who thought through how to frame the issue to the group gathered, who needed to be there, who needed to speak and who directed the discussion in a way that put them in position to be led by the Holy Spirit. Although it was intense at times, it was not a free-for-all.

As the agenda takes shape, the discernmentarian needs to make sure that the group is prepared with as much information as possible—background and financial information, proposals, statistics, research or pertinent readings. This should be distributed ahead of time so the members have time to read and digest it before coming to the meeting. Anticipating the kinds of questions that might be raised in the discussion, the leader should have pertinent information ready in case it is needed. If there are voices that need to be heard in addition to those of the discernment group, the discernmentarian needs to arrange to have these individuals present at the appropriate time.

LISTEN TOGETHER

When the group gathers, begin by briefly reiterating the question for discernment and recounting the circumstances that have brought this question to the fore—it might be something disturbing (such as a financial loss or shortfall, a moral failing, burnout, lack of productivity by someone in leadership, declining attendance) or something that feels very much like a work of the Spirit (an explosion of church or ministry growth, new ministry opportunities, a potential partnership, financial gift or surplus). Even if everyone has come into the meeting knowing what the issue is, bring renewed focus by making sure that everyone involved has the same information, is apprised of any new developments and is clear that there are no secrets or hidden agendas.

> Start with the narrative of the group's process to this point. The group needs to hear how God has worked so far. . . .
>
> If a committee already has spent time sorting out the issues and answering questions, summarize the process the committee went through. . . . Trace the work of the committee for the larger group so that everyone can see how the committee thought about important issues; many of these discussions don't need to be duplicated in the larger group. Bring the group in on the thoroughness and thoughtfulness of the group's process![1]

Then, invite questions for clarification to make sure everyone has the information they need to listen well. This way, everyone starts out on equal footing and there is a trustful, open attitude.

Don't take it for granted that people know how to listen. We live in a culture where people are much more skilled at trying to get their point across and arguing their position than they are at engaging in mutually influencing relationships. The following are a few guidelines for entering into and maintaining a listening posture that helps us hear and interact in ways that are most fruitful.

1. Take full advantage of the opportunity provided to become settled in God's presence.

2. Listen to others with your entire self (senses, feelings, intuition, imagination and rational faculties).

3. Do not interrupt.

4. Pause between speakers to absorb what has been said.

5. Do not formulate what you want to say while someone else is speaking.

6. Speak for yourself, expressing your own thoughts and feelings, referring to your own experiences. Avoid being hypothetical. Steer away from making broad generalizations.

7. Do not challenge what others say. Rather, ask good questions that enable you to wonder about things together.

8. Listen to the group as a whole—to those who have spoken aloud as well as to those who haven't. If you notice that someone hasn't spoken, feel free to ask what he or she is thinking. Some people aren't as comfortable as others at asserting themselves in conversation, but when space is created for them to speak, they have much to offer because they have been listening and observing quietly.

9. Leave space for anyone who may want to speak a first time before speaking a second time yourself.

10. Hold your desires and opinions—even your convictions—lightly. Be willing to be influenced by others whom you respect.[2]

You might also find it helpful to adopt a prayer that helps you settle into a listening stance—one in which you specifically ask God to help you listen well and hear him through the things that

will be shared. Use it to usher yourself into the listening portion
of your meeting. Here is one of my favorites:

> Grant, O God, that we may wait patiently,
> as servants standing before their lord,
> to listen and know your will;
> that we may welcome all truth,
> under whatsoever outward forms it may be uttered;
> that we may bless every good deed, by whomsoever it may
>   be done;
> and that, rising above all strife and contention,
> we may contemplate your eternal truth and goodness,
> through Jesus Christ our Savior. Amen.[3]

Personal Reflection

*How do you relate to the kind of listening described here? Invite
God to search you and reveal your normal patterns of speaking
and listening. Ask him to reveal one aspect of this kind of listening that you could practice in order to be a more helpful
listener in leadership discernment.*

GATHER INFORMATION AND NOTICE WITHOUT JUDGING

The initial move of the listening phase of the discernment process
is to *gather as much data as possible.* Use the following in order to
notice everything without judging.

- *Pertinent facts and information.* Gather background information,
  financial reports and implications, pertinent research and statistics, actual proposals, advice from experts and so forth.

- *Voices from the community.* Listen to those who will be affected by our decision, those who will carry out our decision
  and those who have a special anointing, giftedness, expe-

rience or expertise in the area we are discussing. Pay attention to long-term members of the community who have special wisdom (sage); the Quakers call this "weightiness." This is someone who has a level of spiritual maturity and experience that gives his or her voice strength. The strength of this person's voice might be applicable to most issues, but it could also apply to particular issues in which this person has unusually helpful experience and sensitivity.[4] Peter's voice had particular weight in the Acts 15 story because he was anointed by God to reach Gentiles.

- *Direction and calling.* What fits best with the direction and calling of God on this church or organization? (It can be helpful to review your mission statement here.)

- *Scripture.* Is God bringing to mind Scripture that has direct bearing on what we are discussing? Do the larger themes of Scripture provide a context for this decision?

- *The life of Christ.* Is there anything in the life and teachings of Jesus that informs our considerations? Does this decision reflect the mind of Christ as described in Philippians 2?

- *Fruit of the Spirit.* Read through the fruit of the Spirit in Galatians 5:22-26. Which choice will nurture the fruit of the Spirit in our community? What is our growing edge as a community? Which choice will give God the greatest opportunity to continue his transforming work in us?

- *Consolation and desolation.* Which alternative brings us the deepest sense of life (Jn 10:10), inner peace (Phil 4:7), freedom in the Spirit (2 Cor 3:17)? Which brings us a sense of wholeness, authenticity, congruence with who we are in God? Which choice fosters a deeper level of surrender to God and to love? Which would draw us away from God? Pay particular attention to distress, confusion and desolation.

Even the more difficult emotions need to be acknowledged and attended to.

- *Tradition.* Is there a guiding principle or deep wisdom contained in our faith tradition, our denominational tradition or our community history (particularly the wisdom and charism of our founders) that could give guidance?

- *Love and unity.* Since our ability to love one another and to come together in unity is Jesus' desire for us and glorifies him, which alternative would foster the greatest unity among us? Since love is our highest calling, what is the most loving thing we could do—for God, for ourselves, for our brothers and sisters in Christ, for those we are called to serve?

Obviously, some of these questions and areas of listening and discussion (like pertinent facts and information, various voices that need to be heard) will be foundational for the discernment process. Others will seem especially relevant to the particular issue being processed. These suggestions are not to be seen as a grocery list to be checked off or an academic assignment to be completed. Create space for different people in the group to be drawn to different questions that seem particularly pertinent to this process and that come out of their own attentiveness to what's going on. It could be that in prayer and preparation, the discernmentarian felt other questions would be particularly helpful and has worked those into the agenda.

Personal Reflection

Which one of these questions are you drawn to relative to the issue your group is discerning? Why?

These questions can be seen as on-ramps into the kind of discussions that are most fruitful for discernment. Many of them are interconnected, so one will quite naturally lead to others. Any one of these questions will take you where you need to go—onto the main road of the spiritual conversations that are needed in order for discernment to occur.

LISTEN IN SILENCE

After you have listened together, there are several things that might happen, and silence is the appropriate response to all of them. One possibility is that *a solution might start to become clear* to the group and someone is able to name it. That's fine. Do not shy away from this, but don't rush to make this happen. Keep in mind, however, that "way opening" (as the Quakers would characterize it) or having someone in the group graced with the ability to synthesize what is happening so that the group gets a glimpse of the way forward (like James) is very different from brainstorming and working hard to come up with a human solution. Learning how to tell the difference is important (this will be discussed later). If some clarity opens up in the group, receive it; it will be part of what everyone takes into silence. Silence will provide an opportunity for God to confirm it, reveal more, or raise additional questions and concerns. Encourage people to listen, in particular, to consolation and desolation around whatever they have heard.

Another possibility is that *people will feel overwhelmed or confused* by all that has been presented or by the complexity of the issues. Not sure which direction to go or what to do, they are experiencing the reality of matters that are "too great and too marvelous for me." This is uncomfortable but also wonderful! Don't fight this feeling. When the group feels the limits of its own wisdom and resources, it creates room for God to work. "Blessed are the poor in spirit, for theirs is the kingdom of heaven" (Mt 5:3). The temptation is to keep talking at this point, but silence is the only place you should go with it. It takes discipline to call for silence when everyone is riled up.

A third possibility is that the group might *start moving too quickly into a frenzy of problem solving, brainstorming, arguing and thinking hard.* This can degenerate into a conversation in which human dynamics are more at work than spiritual ones. This is not to say that rigorous discussion is bad; after all, the Jerusalem Council definitely had moments of dissension, debate and differing points of view. We want all points of view to be aired and all the different positions to have fully interacted with each other. The way ahead could be a synthesis of the best aspects of several points of view.

But beware the moment when these human dynamics start getting out of control. This might come as a sense that there have been too many words, people are no longer listening well or are starting to repeat themselves, and the process is just plain stuck. The discernmentarian's role is very important here because when this starts to happen, it's time to go into silence. It is the leader's job to call the group into silence.

WHY SILENCE HELPS

Discernment requires self- and other-awareness as well as space for the Holy Spirit to work. Silence creates space for this. In silence we can become aware of our emotions, thoughts, experiences, sins, temptations, attachments and places where we are not indifferent so that we can see how it affects our participation and take responsibility for ourselves. With a little bit of distance, we also might be able to observe group dynamics and name them in a way that is helpful, which may open up the possibility of change. Most of all, silence leads us to an awareness of others and the gift they are to us—in our sameness and in our diversity. In silence we return to a place of honoring each other and the complexity of the situation.

Silence helps us cease striving so we can rest in God. It brings calm to the inner chaos we might be feeling. Silence creates space for us to deal with our own inner dynamics and listen to God—which is often what is most needed. Silence is an occasion for asking, What needs to die in me in order for the will of God to come forth? What is it in me that is causing this intensity, this fighting spirit, this need to keep such a tight grip on my own opinion? This can be a powerful interruption of negative relating patterns and may loosen the grip that false patterns have on people, creating a new kind of momentum. It's sort of like a coach calling for a time-out when the other team is gaining momentum. In the discernment process a "time-out" can interrupt the negative human dynamics and change the momentum. When false-self patterns are out of control, it is possible that the evil one is working to thwart our ability to discern. Silence is the needed time-out that allows God to interrupt the negative momentum and change the way we're playing the game.

Silence at this point creates space to listen within for God's wisdom regarding the outer listening we have been doing. In a normal meeting, allot fifteen to twenty minutes for silence. Let people leave the room to walk or find a place of quiet. If you are at the end of your allotted meeting time, ask people to take some time in silence between now and the next meeting in order to listen to God. If you are on retreat, allow thirty minutes to an hour for people to rest quietly in their rooms, sit in a chapel or other quiet spot, or go for a walk.

Since we do most of our Transforming Center board meetings in a retreat format, we try to get the listening portion of our deliberations done by the end of the evening so members can take all that they've heard into their rest and morning quiet time before reconvening as a group. We are encouraged to use this time for prayer, journaling, exercising, paying attention to consolation or desolation, uncovering an important question, or being directed by God to Scripture or to an image or a metaphor that helps make sense of things.

While everything in you might be screaming to just keep banging away at solutions through normal means, don't do it! The most amazing breakthroughs take place after people have been in silence. Trust the process. Trust God *in* the process. Trust the power of silence.

> For God alone my soul waits in silence;
>> from him comes my salvation. (Ps 62:1)

In the movie *Of Gods and Men,* a group of French monks living in a country besieged by terrorists needed to discern whether to stay in the monastery and remain faithful to their vows to each other and the community they were serving, or leave in order to save their lives. It was an excruciating dilemma. If they stayed they certainly would be killed. If they left they would be abandoning their calling. They were not in agreement. Some felt strongly about staying, others disagreed, and some were undecided. All points of view were expressed with respect and restraint. As they entered into silence and prayerful listening, their leader dismissed them with these simple words, "Our help comes from the Lord," and the brothers responded, "Who made heaven and earth." What a perfect way to enter into silence—by affirming who and what we are seeking in the silence.

Leader: *Our help comes from the Lord,*
Response: *Who made heaven and earth.*

If we center down . . . and live in that holy Silence which is dearer than life, and take our life program into the silent places of the heart, with complete openness, ready to do, ready to renounce according to His leading, then many of the things we are doing lose their vitality for us. . . . There is a reevaluation of much that we do or try to do . . . and we know what to do and what to let alone.

THOMAS KELLY, *A TESTAMENT OF DEVOTION*

RECONVENE AND LISTEN AGAIN

The words that follow these times of silence are often characterized by deeper wisdom and truer insight than previously. So, after the allotted time for silence, reconvene the group and speak to one another out of the silence. The group will probably gather a little more quietly than usual. Start by asking what happened for them and what God said to them in the silence. These two questions create space for important insights to be shared. The question about what happened for them can be fruitful because it encourages group members to share what they noticed about themselves and what shifts might have taken place.

For instance, someone might say, "When I first went into the silence, I noticed that I was all riled up and had a hard time settling down. There was a part of me that wanted to keep fighting and arguing. However, when I was able to let go of my desire to fight and became a little more quiet on the inside, God started showing me the ways I try to control outcomes rather than trusting him for what's needed. I realize now that it was because of my desire to be in control that I challenged so-and-so rather than really listening. In the silence I realized that there is real wisdom in what so-and-so was saying, and I think we need to consider it."

Someone else might say, "In silence I realized that even though the idea we're considering makes sense strategically, it just exhausts me. Everything in me wants to run the other way! As I stayed with that feeling of exhaustion, I realized I was experiencing desolation because I am already at my limit in terms of time and energy. Even though it's a great idea, I can't imagine being able to do all the work that it would involve for each of us personally and for our community as a whole."

Another person might come back having experienced God's leading to consider a particular passage of Scripture and invite the group to reflect on its relevance to the issue they are facing. Someone else may have been given an image or a metaphor that helps make sense of the situation they are looking at. Or a business person might have been gifted by God with an innovative business model or fundraising idea that will help with the financial side of the question. We never know what will come from these times of silence, but something always does. God works with individuals in silence, yet their contributions come together in ways that no one could have imagined.

At this point it is likely that a way forward—or even a couple of options—begins to emerge. If so, the group moves to the next place in the process.

SELECT AN OPTION CONSISTENT
WITH WHAT GOD IS DOING

In some cases the way forward will present itself clearly and quickly, as happened in Acts 15. After James described his own conviction that beyond the basics of abstaining from things polluted by idols and fornication, "we should not trouble those Gentiles who are turning to God," the whole group affirmed this as God's way forward. Confirming this decision was the widespread experience of peace and unity it brought among the Christians of Jerusalem and Antioch:

- "The apostles and the elders, with the consent of the whole church" (v. 22)

- "we have decided unanimously" (v. 25)

- "it has seemed good to the Holy Spirit and to us" (v. 28)

- "when the members read it [the letter communicating the decision of the council] they rejoiced" (v. 31)

- "they were sent off in peace" (v. 33)

Peace and unity are two markers indicating that God's will has indeed been discerned.

Discernment does not always come with as much clarity, but do not despair! When the way forward is not clear, select an option or two and seek to improve those options so they are the best they can possibly be. The discernmentarian can serve the group by clearly articulating the best options the group has identified. Perhaps the options can be posted on newsprint so everyone can work on them together. When these options have been clearly articulated for the group, give a moment or two of silence for the members to reflect on them quietly. Then draw the group into a conversation in which you seek to (1) notice and name the good in each option, (2) improve on each option, or (3) combine what is best from each option to form a third and better option. Honestly listing the advantages and disadvantages of each option can also be very helpful at this point.

By now the whole group has so thoroughly worked on the options that no one can take sole ownership of any particular option. Now the full energy and focus of the group is on working together to find the best way forward for the group and the community it represents.

Now the discernmentarian can summarize the group's progress by clearly stating the option (or options) and inviting the group to respond. "Does the way I have stated the option (or options) accurately capture what we have discussed? Is anyone uncomfortable with proceeding to the next step?" If someone does express discomfort, make adjustments as needed before proceeding.

WEIGHING THE OPTION(S)

The discernment group is now invited to weigh the option(s) to examine what is most consistent with what God is doing among them; the process is coming to conclusion! The Quaker tradition encourages folks to "place each path near the heart" to see if it brings consolation or desolation. Does the Spirit of God seem to rest on this option? What is the fruit of this option? Other questions may be asked: Is there a Scripture that God brings to mind which is pertinent to the issue we are facing? What is God making natural and easy? What brings a sense of lightness and peace even

in the midst of challenge? Is there an option that enables us to do
something before we do everything?

Discernment at this level takes a great deal of psychological
and spiritual maturity because we are expecting leaders to pay attention to consolation and desolation as more than just surface
emotions. And we are asking them to use this knowledge respon-
sibly. You can begin to see why the ability to discern together "depends greatly on our spiritual and psychological maturity," as we
discussed in chapter three.[5]

AGREE TOGETHER

Once the leadership group has thoroughly explored the option
(or options) and dealt with questions that the group has raised,
clarity should begin to emerge. This is when those who are responsible for discerning and doing the will of God look at each
other and say, "To the best of our ability, we agree that this particular path is God's will for us. So this is the direction we will
go." It is the leader's job to articulate for the group "the sense of
the meeting"—the conclusion to which God seems to be leading
them. Then the question is, Does this matter need more prayer
and reflection? Or are we ready to close by agreeing together on
the way forward?

If the group is ready to respond, ask whether each member affirms that the articulated path seems to be God's will to the best
of his or her ability to discern it. This step is extremely important
because it allows each person to speak his or her true mind and
heart on the matter so the group can move forward in unity. It
safeguards the unity of the group by avoiding future arguments
about whether there really was agreement. It also prevents anyone
from sowing seeds of doubt later on by saying, "Well, I wasn't
really sure, but I didn't want to say anything."

Whatever successes come as a result of this decision, everyone
celebrates together. And whatever challenges come, everyone faces

those together. There can be no finger pointing and blaming. Whatever we did, we did it together.

In the Quaker tradition "unity is the fundamental marker that God's direction has been discerned."[6] The frequently stated objective of "the sense of the meeting" is about unity, rather than unanimity or consensus. Friends find unity on what is best *for the community meeting on this particular issue,* even though they may disagree on the particulars of the issue at hand. Unity requires all to reach the same conclusion about what should be done in the name of all, even when opinions still differ. They believe that what is more important than the decision itself is the quality of their life together. This is not unity that comes from simple giving in on important matters of conscience; it is, rather, a spirit of unity that God gives to his people as they seek him together. The priority of this kind of unity is something all of us would do well to consider before, during and as we look back upon any discernment process.

That said, there are several levels of agreement that can signify unity of spirit:

- Everyone in the circle unequivocally agrees.

- "I agree but with some reservation; however, I have expressed my reservations and feel I have been heard by the group, so I can go forward in peace."

- "I don't agree, but I feel comfortable deferring to those who have particular wisdom, who are most affected, who have greater certainty."

- "No, I don't agree and cannot go forward. In order for me to agree, we will need to go back to the drawing board, wait and pray."

All of these responses are very respectful of the group and give priority to unity of *spirit* even when there might be differences of *opinion.* When someone who is respected in leadership (and hopefully all members of the group are) communicates doubt, this will send the group back into discernment mode. Do not see this as a sign of failure. See this person's thoughtful resistance and willingness to speak the truth as a gift to the group. This can spur the group on to fine-tune their discernment, or it might be seen as a potential safeguard against an unwise decision. At the very least there is something God still wants to reveal to the group through this person's inability to agree.

SEEK INNER CONFIRMATION IN PEACE

The final move is to give everyone the space to seek *inner* confirmation of the decision. Sometimes in the excitement of a meeting we can get carried away by what is happening at the moment; a herd mentality can set in. It is important to allow members some time apart from the group to become quiet in God's presence, to pray and think through what has taken place, and to notice whether they are truly at peace with the decisions being made.

So, take a break and then come back together to check in and see what God is saying to each member of the group. Depending on your time frame, this can be a fifteen to twenty minute break in an evening meeting, an hour or overnight if you are on retreat, or even the week or the month between meetings. When you get back together, if everyone experienced deep, inner peace with the agreed-on option, then affirm that together. If anyone is still having reservations or is experiencing doubts, honor him or her by listening and being open to what God has to say through them. Perhaps one element of a particular option needs to be tweaked, or perhaps a larger adjustment needs to be made. Trust God to work through each person's hesitation or wholehearted affirmation at this point.

If the new direction has been confirmed in each person's spirit, then move forward by affirming the decision in the group and within the wider community. Depending on your church polity or organizational structure, it might be appropriate to share your discernment *process* (not just the outcome) with the community. Invite their input and affirmation as well. Involving the larger community in discernment and how we communicate decisions are matters for discernment as well. However you choose to do this, the fact that leaders have taken such care to discern God's will and have experienced and preserved unity in the process should be a cause for great celebration in the larger community!

In Community

PRACTICING TOGETHER

As a group, work through the final moves in the discernment process. Depending on your meeting rhythms and the magnitude of the issue you are facing, you may work in chapters ten and eleven for a while. Because you are still learning them—not by reading *about* them but by experiencing them—the moves may seem a bit ponderous the first time you go through them.

Though experiential learning takes longer than "book learning," it is much more effective in the end. After you have used the discernment process a few times, the steps will become familiar and will flow so naturally that you will not have to focus on them. Be patient during your initial foray through the moves and learn everything you can. Nothing will be lost, and everything you learn will serve you in future seasons of discernment.

Finish with this closing prayer of thanksgiving. The italic parts are read by all.

CLOSING PRAYER
A Prayer of Thanksgiving

And now let the peace of Christ rule in our hearts,
to which indeed we are called in one body.
And let us be thankful.

Accept, O Lord, our thanks and praise for all you have done for us.
We thank you for setting us at tasks which demand our best efforts,
and for leading us to accomplishments which satisfy and delight us.

We thank you for those disappointments and failures
that lead us to acknowledge our dependence on you alone.

Above all, we thank you for your Son Jesus Christ;
for the truth of his Word and the example of his life;
for his steadfast obedience, by which he overcame temptation;
for his dying, through which he overcame death;
and for his rising to life again, in which we are
raised to the life of your kingdom.

Grant us the gift of your Spirit, that we may know Christ
and make him known;
And through him, at all times and in all places,
may give thanks to you in all things.
Amen.[7]

But Does It Work?

Whoever does the will of God is my brother and sister and mother.

JESUS

❧

The Grace Church group was ready to discern a real issue they were facing. The pastoral staff and elders gathered for a time of retreat—a group of about twenty-five people altogether. There was a good spirit in the group, but elders and staff were quite polarized on the decision they were trying to make. Part of the reason for the lack of agreement was that the outcome would create much more work for the staff. The senior pastor and the elders had already had quite a few "energized" conversations about it, so they definitely were not neutral as they entered the process.

During the first night the facilitator guided the group through the initial session on personal spiritual preparation and established the rhythm of fixed-hour prayer for their time together. After Night Prayer they moved into silence for personal solitude and then to bed. She encouraged them to pay attention to their level of indifference to anything but the will of God, and to begin praying the prayer for indifference relative to the issue they were discerning.

The next day they had Morning Prayer and then reviewed the teaching on cultivating community at the leadership level and the commitment they had made to each other in that regard. Since emotions had been running high, it was good to go back over these things. In the late morning they got started with the early stages of discernment: clarifying the question, checking in with each other about indifference, praying for wisdom and settling into the prayer of quiet trust.

After Midday Prayer and lunch, they gathered for the "listening to each other" portion of the process. For the next couple of hours, all points of view were expressed honestly, thoroughly and at times with great emotion and rigorous back-and-forth interactions—especially between the senior pastor and the elders. That took until about three in the afternoon. Then they went into solitude until dinnertime. Their instructions were to rest, examine a list of questions provided (see pp. 208-10) to see which they were drawn to, and listen to whatever God had to say. As they departed to go into silence, the situation was unresolved and many wondered if there was any hope for unity on this issue.

That evening, they reconvened for Evening Prayer and dinner. As the sun went down, the group brought their coffee and tea into the parlor where they had been having their teaching sessions. A candle was lit to symbolize their intent to allow the Holy Spirit to guide them, and then they "listened again"—this time to what had come out of their time of silence. They went around the room giving everyone the opportunity to share how God had led them in their solitude, and it was an amazing experience of seeing the Holy Spirit move through the group. *Every person* had come to the same conclusion through a different interior journey clearly guided by the Spirit. In fact, several key people had been led *to the same Scripture passage*—even though they had not talked to each other all afternoon.

When there were still a few people to hear from, the group was aware that God was working far beyond anything they could have imagined. A hush descended on the room. As the last people shared and everyone realized that there was unanimity on an issue where there had been such polarization, they sat in stunned silence; tears ran down many faces. After a time, they ended the session and went to Night Prayer—glad that they had someplace to go with all that had happened. They had dessert after that, and quite a celebration it was!

The next morning their conversation centered on logistics and how they would carry out the will of God as they had discerned it. When they made the announcement to the congregation, informing them *how the decision had been made* and the level of unity that had been achieved, the congregation jumped to their feet and cheered. There was an amazing sense that the decision was good, but what pleased everyone most was the sense of unity *the process* had fostered. It had been a long time since they had experienced that kind of unity on such a large scale. In what was becoming one of the highlights of their life together in community, they looked forward to actually *doing* the will of God they had discerned.

JUST DO IT!

The main point of discerning the will of God is to do it. Once a leadership group feels they have discerned the will of God to the best of their ability, it is time to move forward into the planning and implementation phases with confidence that "the one who has called you will be faithful to bring it to pass" (see 1 Thess 5:24). This is the time to bring in the consultants and the strategic planners, if needed—those who can help the group do the will of God with wisdom and excellence. This is the time to connect the dots between prayerful discernment and Spirit-empowered action. And part of connecting the dots is to make good decisions about how to best communicate what has been discerned with others who need to know.[1]

This was the next step for the Jerusalem Council once they had discerned the will of God (Acts 15). After James articulated what God was doing among them (v. 19) and the apostles and elders along with the whole congregation affirmed it (vv. 22, 25, 28), it was time to think through how to communicate and carry it out effectively. Moving into planning mode, they decided to choose respected individuals to accompany Paul and Barnabas as they carried a letter to the Christians in Antioch that explained the council's decision (vv. 23-29). Their strategy worked! The Antioch Christians rejoiced at what their leaders had discerned, and they were strengthened and encouraged by the teaching that was brought to them. The care that the Jerusalem Council took to discern God's will strengthened the whole community.

THE SACRED RHYTHM OF MINISTRY

Establishing a rhythm of *discerning* and *doing* the will of God moves us beyond the false dichotomies between being and doing, prayer and action, and spiritual transformation and engaging the world. We experience the fact that the best *doing* emerges from our *being* in God, our most effective *action* emerges from our *prayer*, and our most loving *engagement with the world* comes as a direct result of *Christ's love and compassion being formed in us*. Our spiritual transformation results in the ability to discern loving and wise action in the world.

Once God's will has been discerned, it is important to act on it in a spirit of ongoing discernment. Many things still need to be discerned about how to carry out the will of God. If the physical plant is to be expanded, discernment is needed about the general contractor, finances, fundraising and what to do if the funds don't come through. If it's ministry expansion, how will it be done while maintaining a pace of life that fosters healthy spiritual rhythms? If an individual discerns a change in his or her participation that will affect the group, how will this be communicated and carried out with love and regard for everyone involved?

Resist the urge to get carried away in all the excitement of having discerned God's will; move forward in doing God's will with a continued commitment to discernment.

Every genuine expression of love grows out of a consistent and total surrender to God.

MARTIN LUTHER KING JR., *STRENGTH TO LOVE*

HOLD IT LOOSELY

The process of leadership discernment is one of the most demanding and yet exhilarating aspects of spiritual leadership. When a leadership group starts making decisions in this fashion, the stress of making major decisions subsides. Our joy in community and confidence in God's intimate presence increases dramatically. Discernment becomes a source of ongoing inspiration; we grow to love it and rely on it. However, a word of caution: embracing the leadership discernment process should not be followed slavishly or with an obsessive-compulsive attachment to rule keeping—as though discernment can't happen unless we follow the steps exactly.

Sometimes meetings and processes do not go exactly as we have planned, and yet we can trust that the Spirit of God is able to visit us and give us the gifts of wisdom and discernment. When individuals of the leadership community are functioning in a state of ongoing spiritual preparedness, discernment is attainable even when extenuating circumstances or time constraints interfere with the ideal.

I remember one such board meeting when we had an important hiring decision to make and just could not keep to the agenda I had set—which included time for fixed-hour prayer and the process described in this book. A major snowstorm prevented one of our board members from flying in as planned (he could only be present by phone). And those who drove arrived a full two hours late. I was resolved to abide by the agenda and was having a very hard time containing my frustration. Then, right at the time I had marked out for silence, one of our members had to leave for a family emergency. He was willing to remain with us on his cell phone as he drove home but that would be our last half hour together at all.

Given the delays and our inability to be in silence together, all we could do was take those last few minutes to make the decision without going into silence—which I am loathe to do. But I also recognized that I needed to adjust to the reality of the situation and trust that the Holy Spirit would still lead us. And that is exactly what happened. With two board members on phones and only a half hour left in much less than ideal circumstances, we stayed with it and stayed with each other; in that half hour we came to a profound level of agreement on the course of action we needed to take. It turned out that a Scripture passage read in Morning Prayer had particular relevance to the question we were discerning, and one of our board members drew our attention to it in a way that led us to great clarity.

We were very grateful for the way the Holy Spirit had guided us even though we could not adhere to our normal practice of leadership discernment, and we learned that God does not need our disciplines in order to find us. We need discipline in order to bring some structure to our intent to open ourselves to God—alone and together. Our desire and intent is what we bring, and God does the rest.

ONE LEADER'S STORY

Right about now you might be feeling a number of emotions. Dismayed that you have not been leading through a discernment process. Exhilarated at the possibility of leading together with others in this new way. Burdened by doubts about whether it will work in your setting. The following story is testimony to the power and efficacy of leadership discernment—even when we feel overwhelmed and inexperienced—from Rev. David Hughes, senior pastor of First Baptist Church, a large, historic church in Winston-Salem, North Carolina. He has given me permission to share this story in his own words.

Years ago I remember watching the doctor who invented the "Heimlich Maneuver" demonstrate the procedure on television. A few days later my wife and I were eating at a banquet with a friend who suddenly began choking on a bite of food. As our friend slowly turned blue in the face, my wife urged me to do something, anything to save our friend. In desperation I hastily performed the Heimlich maneuver, all the while thinking, *I cannot imagine this is really going to work.* Much to my amazement and relief, it did. The food became dislodged, and our friend lives on to this day!

That experience is much like what happened when I left my first "discernment retreat" with the Transforming Center a few years ago. The teachings that were presented excited me. And scared me. And depressed me. And beyond that, I couldn't imagine that it would really work!

I was excited because for the first time in my thirty years of ministry I had heard someone offer an in-depth presentation of personal and leadership discernment, soundly rooted in both Scripture and Christian tradition. I was scared because making decisions through discernment rather than simply through the rational processes I was accustomed to would push me *way* out of my comfort zone. And I was depressed by the thought that I had been missing the mark so clearly as I made decisions in my own life, not to mention how I led the congregation I pastored in decision making.

Yes, God in his grace had guided me in the past despite myself. But I wanted to do better, both in my personal life and in my ministry. Now I knew I could. Little did I know I would soon have the opportunity to put my new learnings about discerning together as leaders into practice.

A few days after returning from that soul-stretching retreat about discernment as the heart of spiritual leadership, I was contacted by the chair of a search committee in our congregation who were seeking a new staff member. The committee had become dead-locked around two candidates, according to the chair. Every attempt to end the stalemate had failed, and the committee wondered if I would come and advise them about how to proceed.

Of course, I agreed to attend the next meeting, though I was clueless about how to help. Then my mind turned to what I had just learned a few days earlier. Should I share the material I learned at the discernment retreat with this struggling committee?

I remember sitting with the committee in a member's home on a cold winter's night, a fire roaring in the fire place. I remember telling the committee about my retreat experience, and how I had learned some things that might be helpful. I began by reminding them of the Quaker belief that unity within a body is a clear sign of the work of the Holy Spirit in the body of Christ. I asked them not to come to our church with a divided recommendation about this staff position (as had happened in past searches), but to continue working with one another until some semblance of unity was achieved.

I walked them through the steps of corporate discernment, and spent considerable time explaining the attitude and prayer of indif-ference. I led them through a time of listening and prayer. Ever so slowly, I could feel the tension in the room melt—and not just be-cause of the roaring fire.

Truthfully, I shared this material out of desperation, not knowing what else to say. And I confess thinking to myself, *I cannot imagine that this is really going to work!*

As the meeting drew to a conclusion, I recommended the com-mittee call it a night and allow members to pray and meditate over their decision before reconvening. They did. And after their follow-up meeting, the committee chair called, ecstatic that the com-mittee had reached a unanimous decision about a candidate to recommend. What was stunning about the chair's enthusiasm is that the candidate that eventually emerged was not the one she had favored just a few days before!

Needless to say, the "discernment stuff" worked. Our church went on to hire the recommended candidate, and that hire has proven to be one of the best in my twenty years of ministry in this church! Since then, we have used the practice of leadership discernment to help us decide other issues. We are not experts in discernment—far from it. Indeed, these days we are focused on developing the *habit* of discernment as a precursor to the practice of discernment. But we cannot and will not go back to the old decision-making model of beginning with a brief prayer, conducting a logic-based (though often emotionally heated) discussion loosely governed by Robert's Rules of Order, taking a vote (usually creating "winners and losers"), and ending with an even briefer ("How quickly can we get out of here?") concluding prayer.

There is, after all, a much better and far more biblical way.

NEXT STEPS FOR YOUR COMMUNITY

So, how are you feeling as you come to the end of this book? Are you inspired by the idea that you can actually practice discernment together utilizing concrete, practical steps? Are you overwhelmed at what seems to be such a long process to get there? Are you wondering how you might find the time for everything—listening, silence, the space for seeking inner confirmation—and still get through your meeting agendas?

You might also be grappling with the fact that this sort of discernment will require more of you spiritually. More time for silence and prayer in your personal life. Increased commitment to self-knowledge and self-examination. A willingness to die to what is false within you.

If it feels like too much, here is a simple suggestion: let it rest a bit—like yeast in a lump of dough—and see how God speaks to you about what you have learned. During the next several months, keep working on staying true to your spiritual rhythms, and notice the changes that are taking place among your group. Take time in your next leadership meeting to identify one or two elements of the process you can realistically incorporate into your leadership process. Then, try introducing one or two aspects of discernment into the process of making the decisions you are facing.

- Are you drawn to try fixed-hour prayer?

- Could you introduce a little bit of silence for listening to God after the information about a decision has been fully shared?

- Do you feel safe enough with each other to introduce the test for indifference before you enter into the heart of the discernment process?

- Is there someone on your team you could trust with facilitating the discernment process, or do you need to invite someone from outside the group to hold the process in place?

- Could you make it a practice to consider what additional voices need to be invited to speak into a particular question or issue you are discerning?

The point is this: Do something before you do everything. Do what you *can* do and be assured that God is faithful to come into any amount of space we create for him. Rest in the knowledge that

the LORD waits to be gracious to you;
    therefore he will rise up to show mercy to you.
For the LORD is a God of justice;
    blessed are all those who wait for him. . . .

Your Teacher will not hide himself any more, but your eyes shall see your Teacher. And when you turn to the right or when you turn to the left, your ears shall hear a word behind you, saying, "This is the way; walk in it." (Is 30:18, 20-21)

In Community

PRACTICING TOGETHER

Take time now as a group to talk about your convictions and your commitment to pursuing God's will together. Where are the places of resonance and resistance? Be honest about the challenges and opportunities that are unique to the particularities of your situation—your history, your church polity, your meeting patterns, the mix of people in your leadership group. How is God leading you to move forward with becoming a community for discernment so you can pursue God's will together?

CLOSING PRAYER

O God our Wisdom, who eternally makes all things new;
encourage by your Holy Spirit
those of us who seek to discern your will
that we may labor together for the building up of your world
and your Church;
counsel us when to act and when to wait;
turn our hearts always toward those in greatest need,
and away from our own preoccupations and fears;
help us never to forget that love and mercy are your
greatest gifts, given us all to offer one another
as we see in them Jesus Christ
who alone
is our joy, our way, our truth, and our life.
Amen.[2]

GRATITUDES

For all that has been, thank you. For all that is to come, yes.

DAG HAMMARSKJÖLD

Someone has said that life is what happens while you are planning to do something else. I have discovered that God's will is like that too. Three years ago, when I made plans (and signed a contract) to write this book, I didn't have any grandchildren; now I have three—grandsons to be exact! This book is dedicated to these precious little boys in celebration of God's will in my life which is better than anything I could have planned.

It is also dedicated to the leadership community of the Transforming Center, without whom I would not have had a context in which to learn and practice, teach and live the truths contained in this book. While I am the first to admit that we are not perfect, I can say that we *are* a community gathered around the presence of Christ, committed to spiritual transformation so we can discern and do the will of God. For that reason and by God's grace, discernment happens among us more often than not, and each time it does, we receive it and each other as pure gift. As we celebrate ten years of ministry, my heart is full of gratitude to each one who has been part of this great adventure of responding to Christ in our midst. Thanks be to God.

Special thanks are due to Dalene, who so faithfully manages the details of my vocational life and responds to the outside world so that I have any space at all to write. I know it is a cliché but I must say it: I could not do any of this without you.

With the completion of this book, I am particularly aware of my teachers and mentors (some from afar)—Bill Clemmons, Gordon Cosby, Robert Mulholland, Chuck Olsen, Tilden Edwards, Rose Mary Dougherty and Jerry May (deceased)—whose lives and teachings have impacted me so profoundly. You have given so generously of your wisdom, theological understanding and wholehearted endorsement of my work that I hardly know what to say.

And to my friends at IVP—thank you for the spiritual journey we have shared all these years. Thank you for a publishing process that is full of integrity and truth. Thank you for being my publisher through thick and thin.

And finally, I am most grateful to my family . . . to my daughters, Charity, Bethany and Haley—each of whom had major, life-changing events going on in their lives while their mother was writing this book. It has not been easy, but through generous love, patient understanding and careful scheduling we have somehow managed to navigate an amazing convergence of graduations and weddings, births of babies and books without losing each other . . . to my parents and brothers for always watching and praying . . . and to Chris, who understands my passion for learning, teaching and writing and has never begrudged me one thing that my calling has required. I love you all with all my heart.

APPENDIX 1

LEADER'S GUIDE

છે

Following are some words of guidance and encouragement for those who facilitate their leadership group in the process of becoming a community for discernment.

First and most importantly, *take your time.* Be realistic about the amount of time it will take your group to make its way through the book. Let these opportunities for personal reflection and group practice unfold in a way that is unique to your group. Don't feel like there is a right or a wrong way to do this. To be honest, it has taken several years to come to a place of clarity on all the levels described in this book. Be patient and never push your group beyond what they are able.

For optimal benefit I suggest that groups *carve out some time in their normal meetings or take a longer retreat to discuss each portion of the book and engage the group practices.* The book is divided into two parts: part one (chaps. 1-8) deals with becoming a community for discernment, which involves preparing the individual leaders (chaps. 1-3) and preparing the community for discernment (chaps.

4-8). Part two (chaps. 9-12) outlines concrete practices for leadership discernment. You could set aside a whole or a half day to work through chapters as you see fit, or you might choose to work through the book in conjunction with your normally scheduled meetings, discussing and practicing one chapter per meeting.

However you choose to do it, *it is best if individuals read the assigned portion of the book ahead of time* and spend some time with the personal reflection questions scattered throughout each chapter. You might *encourage individuals to start a special notebook or journal for capturing their personal reflections.* They can use these reflections when they are together as a group. This will expedite the group process. When the group gathers, spend the time together discussing the content they have read, sharing their personal reflections and engaging the group practices and exercises at the end of each chapter. The closing prayer at the end of each chapter can be used to pray together and "gather it all up" at the end of your meetings.

If you choose to read and interact with one chapter per regularly scheduled meeting, *decide on the amount of time you will set aside for this purpose in your meeting, but be prepared to take as many sessions as you need in order to complete the work of that chapter.* For instance, if in reading and interacting with the first part of the book, you realize that there is little shared understanding of and practice with personal spiritual disciplines and personal discernment, you may want to take additional time to allow individuals to experience these disciplines in order to establish spiritual rhythms in their lives and become comfortable sharing about them together before moving on. The book *Sacred Rhythms* is a good resource to support this part of the process.

Or if when working with the chapters on guiding values and principles, you discover that it is taking more than one meeting to discuss these thoroughly and capture them in writing, take the extra time you need. If you choose to work with the book in a retreat format I recommend the following format: In the first retreat use the introduction and chapter one as a way of casting vision for discernment as the heart of spiritual leadership and coming to some level of agreement about the group's commitment to becoming a community for discernment. Then you will be in agreement that this process is a worthy investment. You can then cover chapters two and three in a following retreat (especially if spiritual transformation and spiritual disciplines are new to the group) and give everyone a few months to practice and get personal rhythms in place. Then cover chapters four through eight in the next retreat (or in a series of several meetings). Chapters nine through twelve can be explored and practiced in another retreat in the context of a real issue that is facing the group.

If at any point you, as facilitator, feel that you are out of your depth, do not hesitate to bring in a resource person to help with aspects of the process where you feel inadequate or you sense that the group may need more help than you are prepared to give.

However you choose to engage this process, *set the expectation that this will be a year-long process*. There is really no need to rush; anything that is of lasting value takes time. Be assured that God is faithful to enter any space we create for him; wherever you are in the process, you are creating space for God and you will quite naturally become more discerning. This is a time to trust God and be faithful to what he is calling forth among you.

> Trust in the slow work of God.
> We are quite naturally
> impatient in everything to reach the end
> without delay.
> We should like to skip
> the intermediate stages.
> We are impatient of being on the way
> to something unknown,

something new.
And yet it is the law of all progress
that it is made by passing through
some stages of instability—
and that it may take a very long time. . . .

Your ideas mature gradually—
let them grow,
let them shape themselves,
without undue haste.
Don't try to force them on,
as though you could be today
what time (that is to say, grace and
circumstances acting on your own good will)
will make them tomorrow.

Only God could say what this new spirit,
gradually forming within you will be.
Give our Lord the benefit of believing
that his hand is leading you,
and accepting the anxiety
of feeling yourself in suspense and incomplete.[1]

Appendix 2

A Biblical Perspective on Spiritual Transformation

I am . . . in labor until Christ is formed in you.

GALATIANS 4:19 NASB

❦

Since spiritual transformation is a prerequisite to discernment, it is important that your group clearly understands what it is, how it takes place in our lives and its significance to the mission of the church. The following is a brief theological perspective that is grounded in Scripture, animated by a trinitarian approach to the spiritual life and informed by the richness of our Christian heritage. It may be helpful to review this together to see if you can affirm a shared understanding of this important element of becoming a community for discernment.

CHRIST FORMED IN US
Spiritual transformation is the process by which Christ is formed in us for the glory of God, for the abundance of our own lives and

for the sake of others (Rom 8:29; 12:1-2; Gal 4:19). The possibility that humans can be transformed to such an extent that they image Christ is central to the message of the gospel, and therefore it is central to the mission of the church. Spiritual transformation in the lives of redeemed people is a testimony to the power of the gospel, and it results in an increasing capacity to discern and do the will of God (Rom 12:2).

RENEWING THE MIND

It is God's will and delight that we actively resist being conformed to this world and seek instead to be transformed by the renewing of our minds. The Greek word *nous* (translated "mind" in Romans 12:2) includes but goes far beyond intellectual or cognitive knowing. It denotes the seat of reflective consciousness and encompasses a person's faculties of perception and understanding as well as the patterns of feeling, judging and determining that shape our actions and responses in the world. Thus, transformation that brings real change must go beyond information at the cognitive level to full knowledge that affects our deepest inner orientations and trust structures, false-self patterns and obstacles that prevent us from surrendering to God. This kind of change involves teaching about the nature of the Christian life, concrete practices that help us internalize truth and change our response to the world, and community that catalyzes and supports the process.

THE WORK OF THE SPIRIT

Spiritual transformation is something of a paradox in that it is natural and supernatural. Christ followers naturally grow and change just as human beings grow from infancy to childhood to adolescence to adulthood. The seed of the Christ life ("everything needed for life and godliness" [2 Pet 1:3]) is planted within us at salvation, and if the conditions are right, that seed will grow and flourish. But transformation is also supernatural in that it is something only God can accomplish in our lives through the work of the Holy Spirit. The third person of the Trinity is our advocate, teacher and counselor to lead us into truth (Jn 15–16) and to communicate the depths of God (1 Cor 2:9-16). We can find ways to open ourselves to this process of transformation as it is guided by the Spirit, but we cannot control it or make it happen ourselves. The wind of the Spirit blows where it will (Jn 3:8).

Paul alludes to the paradox of the natural and the supernatural by using two metaphors. The first is the process by which an embryo is formed in its mother's womb: "I am . . . in labor until Christ is formed [morphoō] in you" (Gal 4:19 NASB). Even though human beings have their part to play in conceiving and giving birth to children—and even though we think we understand certain facts about it—there is something that remains a mystery. No matter how much we think we understand it, the miracle of birth is always that: a *miracle*. It is something God does. Every single time.

It is the same with the process of metamorphosis, which Paul refers to in Romans 12:2: "Do not be conformed to this world, but be transformed [metamorphoō] by the renewing of your minds." The Greek work *metamorphoō* refers to the process by which, in the darkness of a cocoon, a caterpillar changes into a beautiful butterfly. Through metamorphosis, a caterpillar takes on a completely different form with a completely different set of capacities. The caterpillar's transformation has little to do with cognitive understanding about the process of metamorphosis; something more primal and God-ordained is at work.

EMBRACING MYSTERY
Both the formation of an embryo in its mother's womb and the transformation of a caterpillar in the cocoon are natural phenomena, but they are also God things. This places spiritual transformation squarely in the mystery category—it's outside the range of normal human activity and understanding and can only be understood through divine revelation and brought about by divine

activity. In fact, everything we affirm as central to the Christian journey is referred to as a mystery in Scripture: God (1 Cor 2:1; 4:1); God's will (Eph 1:9); Christ (Eph 3:4); the gospel (Eph 6:19); marriage, which is applied to Christ and the church (Eph 5:31-32); Christ in us, the hope of glory (Col 1:27); Christ himself (Col 2:2); and faith (1 Tim 3:9).

If we are not comfortable with mystery, we are not comfortable with the very gospel we proclaim. The journey of transformation requires willingness to relinquish control and give ourselves over to a process that we cannot fully understand or of which we can predict the outcome. We know we will be more like Christ, but we cannot predict exactly what this will look like or where it will take us.

THE ROLE OF SPIRITUAL DISCIPLINES

While we cannot transform ourselves into the image of Christ, we *can* create the conditions in which spiritual transformation takes place. Like a gardener who prepares for plants to grow by tilling the soil, adding fertilizer and watering, so we can create the conditions that make it possible for the life of Christ to grow and flourish within us. This is where spiritual practices come in. Spiritual practices are not ways to make brownie points with God or to prove our spiritual superiority to others. They are not a self-help program by which we take control of our journey and change ourselves. Rather, spiritual disciplines are concrete activities that we engage in in order to make ourselves available for the work that only God can do. While we cannot transform ourselves into the image of God, we *can* create the conditions in which spiritual transformation can take place.

This is what Paul is referring to when he appeals to the Christians in Rome to "present your bodies as a living sacrifice, holy and acceptable to God, which is your spiritual worship" (Rom 12:1). We can create the conditions for transformation by practicing disciplines that help us surrender to God—not just in theory but in reality. Richard Foster says,

> [Spiritual] disciplines are the main way we offer our bodies up to God as a living sacrifice. We are doing what we can do with our bodies, our minds, our hearts. God then takes this simple offering of ourselves and does with it what we cannot do, producing within us deeply ingrained habits of love and peace and joy in the Holy Spirit.[1]

THE NECESSITY OF COMMUNITY

Spiritual transformation takes place over time with others in the context of disciplines and practices that open us to God. While we still inhabit earth, our transformation will happen by degrees (2 Cor 3:18), and we need each other in order to grow (1 Cor 12).

Paul's teaching on spiritual transformation in Romans 12 and in his epistles is always given in the context of community—the body of Christ with its many members. We are given to one another in the body of Christ for mutual edification and to spur one another on to love and good deeds. Our gifts are not given for our own benefit or self-aggrandizement but so we can be agents of grace for one another, building up the body, of which we are only one part. As Robert Mulholland writes, "We can no more be conformed to the image of Christ outside corporate spirituality than a coal can continue to burn outside of the fire."[2]

While our spiritual practices certainly include private disciplines (solitude and silence, prayer and meditation, Scripture reading, self-examination and confession, retreat, spiritual direction), to be effective they must also include disciplines in community (corporate prayer and worship, teaching, Communion, sabbath, hospitality, caring for those in need, spiritual friendship and direction), and engagement with the world (evangelism, caring for the poor, compassion, justice, etc.).

FOR THE SAKE OF OTHERS

Spiritual transformation is *both* an end in itself, in that it brings glory to God, *and* a means to other ends, in that it enables us to mediate the presence of Christ to others and to discern loving action in the world. The litmus test of mature spirituality is that we are increasing in our capacity to love God and to love others (Mk 12:30-31; 1 Cor 13; 1 Jn 4:7). Loving presence and action in the world includes sharing our faith (evangelism), giving generously of our resources, reconciliation and peacemaking (interpersonally and also across lines of race, gender, socioeconomic status and people groups), working for justice, exercising compassion and care for the poor, and working for the betterment of life in the human community in the name of Jesus.

All true Christian spiritual formation is for the glory of God, for the abundance of our own lives and *for the sake of others*, or it is not *Christian* spiritual formation. For this we toil and struggle with all the energy that God so powerfully inspires within us.

APPENDIX 3

LECTIO DIVINA

&

Lectio divina is an ancient method of reading Scripture that was developed by the desert mothers and fathers to allow God to address them directly through the biblical text. In this approach, we read a short passage of Scripture (no more than six to eight verses) multiple times very slowly; for each consecutive reading there is a simple question designed to take us deeper and deeper into the layers of meaning. Reading Scripture this way helps the Word bypass the cognitive filters we often have in place that can cause us to disregard words or challenging messages that we might want to avoid or are not aware that we need.

Following is a brief description of the lectio divina process. For a full description, see chapter three of *Sacred Rhythms*. You can use passages from the *Revised Common Lectionary, A Guide to Prayer* (Upper Room Publishing) or any chosen passage. Again, it is good to read passages no longer than six to eight verses, unless it's a story.

First, take some time in silence (five to ten minutes) to **prepare** yourself—to quiet your heart and invite God to speak. If you are practicing solitude and silence already, this time can serve as your preparation for engaging Scripture. You may want to pray the prayer Samuel prayed when he was first learning how to recognize God's voice: "Speak, LORD, for your servant is listening" (1 Sam 3:9). You will read the chosen passage four times with time to reflect in silence following each reading.

In the **first reading**, you are invited to listen for the word or phrase that strikes you. This word or phrase might come across as "louder" than the others, or it might resonate with other experiences you've had with the same word. It might also bring tears to your eyes or even cause feelings of resistance. Many people read the passage twice in the first reading to give ample opportunity for receiving the word God wants to give. In the silence that follows, just savor the word or phrase without trying to figure it out or make application connections. After the silence, go around the group and invite members to share the word or phrase they received without comment or discussion. Then go on to the next reading.

In the **second reading**, you are invited to listen for the way in which your life is touched by this word. In the silence that follows, listen to the questions, How is my life touched by this word? What in my life needs to hear this word today? After the silence, go around the circle and allow members to share how their life is touched by this word. Encourage them to share as briefly and succinctly as possible without extra commentary or discussion.

In the **third reading**, you are invited to listen for God's invitation to you. Is there an invitation—something that God is inviting you to do or to be—contained within his word to you? What is your response? Allow for a longer silence so that individuals can interact with God in the quiet of their own heart, hearing God's invitation and then responding honestly to him. After the silence, go around the circle and allow individuals to share what they feel God's invitation to them is from this reading.

In the **fourth reading,** you are invited to rest in God with the word you have received. In the silence that follows, rest in God's ability to bring about whatever it is he is inviting you to do or to be. After the silence, the designated leader can close the whole experience with a brief spoken prayer, thanking God for his presence and his work in each person gathered.

The final move in the lectio process is **resolving to live out or incarnate** the word we have received. We ask, What will it look like for me or for us to "enflesh this word" and live it faithfully?

The desert fathers and mothers often refused or at least hesitated to listen for another word from God until they were fully living out the one they had received. This is a far cry from the way in which we often handle Scripture—galloping through large portions at a time without stopping to hear God speak or wrestle with what it really means for us. There needs to be some balance between reading the Scriptures as a whole so that we understand the broad sweep of God's activity in human history and reading portions small enough that we can dive deep and uncover the layers of its meaning for us. Dietrich Bonhoeffer describes so well the transformative effect of this kind of engagement with Scripture:

> The time of meditation [on Scripture] does not let us down into the void and abyss of loneliness; it lets us be alone with the Word. And in so doing it gives us solid ground on which to stand and clear directions as to the steps we must take. . . .
>
> In our meditation we ponder the chosen text on the strength of the promise that it has something utterly personal to say to us for this day and for our Christian life, that it is not only God's Word for the Church, but also God's Word for us individually. We expose ourselves to the specific word until it addresses us personally. . . . We read God's Word as God's Word for us.[1]

Notes

࿎

Introduction: The Heart of Spiritual Leadership

[1]When I use the word *secular* in this context, I am simply referring to methods that do not acknowledge God or other spiritual dynamics in the process. Certainly there are many good ideas contained in secular models—ideas we can all benefit from. The point here is to make a distinction between decision-making methods that seek God's guidance and those that do not.

Chapter 1: Learning to See

[1]Richard Rohr, *Everything Belongs* (New York: Crossroad, 1999), p. 17.

[2]J. Philip Newell, *Celtic Treasure* (Grand Rapids: Eerdmans, 2005), p. 114.

Chapter 2: Beginning with Spiritual Transformation

[1]For a more thorough treatment of spiritual transformation, spiritual disciplines and guidance for practicing specific disciplines, see Ruth Haley Barton, *Sacred Rhythms: Arranging Our Lives for Spiritual Transformation* (Downers Grove, Ill.: InterVarsity Press, 2006).

[2]For additional guidance, see Ruth Haley Barton, *Invitation to Solitude and Silence*, exp. ed. (Downers Grove, Ill.: InterVarsity Press, 2010).

[3]Dietrich Bonhoeffer, *Life Together* (New York: Harper SanFrancisco, 1954), p. 80.

[4]Parker Palmer, "Leading from Within: Reflections on Spirituality and Leadership," a transcription of an address given at the annual celebration dinner of the Indiana Office for Campus Ministries in March 1990, published by The Servant Leadership School, Washington, D.C., p. 7.

[5]Ibid., p. 8.

[6]Ted Loder, *Guerrillas of Grace* (Philadelphia: Innisfree Press, 1984), p. 86.

Chapter 3: Leaders Who Are Discerning

[1]This quote is actually two very similar quotes combined. The first half of the quote is from Paul Anderson, *With Christ in Decision Making: His Present Leadership Among Friends* (Newberg, Ore.: Barclay Press, 1990), and the second

half is from Paul Anderson, "The Meeting for Worship in Which Business is Conducted," *Quaker Religious Thought* 106-7 (November 2006): 45.

[2]David Benner, *Desiring God's Will* (Downers Grove, Ill.: InterVarsity Press, 2005), p. 14.

[3]Danny Morris and Charles Olsen, *Discerning God's Will Together* (Nashville: Upper Room Books, 1997), p. 42.

[4]Ibid., p. 41.

[5]Ernest Larkin, *Silent Presence* (Denville, N.J.: Dimension Books, 1981), p. 38.

[6]For a more complete treatment of the practice of personal discernment, see chapter 7 of Ruth Haley Barton, *Sacred Rhythms* (Downers Grove, Ill.: InterVarsity Press, 2006).

[7]Morris and Olsen, *Discerning God's Will,* p. 90.

[8]Robert Mulholland unpacks the relationship between indifference and the spiritual discipline of detachment when he writes: "We cannot be indifferent as long as our identity, value, meaning, purpose is attached to something other than God. It is the difficult discipline of detachment that opens us to God so He can nurture in us the posture of indifference. It is what Jesus points us to when he says to Peter, 'Do you love me more than these?' (Jn. 21:15). The 'these' is ambiguous, and I believe purposely so. Whatever we love more than we love Jesus becomes one of the 'soils' for the roots of our false self. Detachment is replacing our love for the 'these' in our lives with love for Jesus. Detachment (asceticism) is the most dangerous of the spiritual disciplines since detachment for any other motive than love for Jesus becomes a subtle delusion of the religious false self which becomes identified by what it is *detached from* rather than *attachment to* Jesus. Yes, we wait for God to make us indifferent but we also need to enter into the discipline of detaching ourselves from those things in our lives which militate against indifference" (from a personal note to the author, December 14, 2011, italics mine).

[9]Timothy M. Gallagher, *Spiritual Consolation: An Ignatian Guide for the Greater Discernment of Spirits* (New York: Crossroad, 2007), p. 23.

[10]Ibid.

[11]Ibid., p. 26.

[12]Thomas Merton, *Spiritual Direction and Meditation,* pp. 16, 17. Copyright 1960, 1987 by Order of Saint Benedict. Published by Liturgical Press, Collegeville, Minnesota. Reprinted with permission.

[13]Ted Loder, *Guerillas of Grace* (Philadelphia: Innisfree Press, 1984), p. 29.

Chapter 4: Community at the Leadership Level

[1]Dietrich Bonhoeffer, *Life Together* (New York: HarperCollins, 1954), pp. 30-31.

[2]John English, *Spiritual Intimacy and Community: An Ignatian View of the Small Faith Community* (New York: Paulist Press, 1992), p. 13.

[3]Ibid., pp. 13, 16.

[4]Reprinted with permission of the publisher. From *Leadership and the New Science,* copyright © 2006 by Margaret J. Wheatley, Berrett-Koehler Publishers, Inc., San Francisco, CA, p. 55. All rights reserved. www.bkconnection.com

[5]Adapted from the Iona Community, *Iona Abbey Worship Book* (Glasgow, U.K.: Wild Goose Publications, 2001), p. 156.

Chapter 5: Values That Undergird Community

[1]Gordon Cosby, *Good Is a Timely Word: From the Preaching of Gordon Cosby* (Nowra, Australia: Moonchpa, 2001), pp. 108-9.

[2]Robert L. Williamson, *Charting Self: The Beliefs Chart as a Tool for Change* (Lombard, Ill.: Lombard Mennonite Peace Center, 2004), p. 4.

[3]K. Killian Noe, *Finding Our Way Home* (Washington, D.C.: Servant Leadership Press, 2001), p. 15.

[4]Elizabeth O'Connor, *Cry Pain, Cry Hope* (Washington, D.C.: The Servant Leadership School, 1987), p. 13.

[5]For a more thorough treatment of how men and women relate to one another in community as brothers and sisters in Christ, see Ruth Haley Barton, *Equal to the Task: Men and Women in Partnership* (Downers Grove, Ill.: InterVarsity Press, 1998).

[6]Robert Mulholland, *Invitation to a Journey* (Downers Grove, Ill.: InterVarsity Press, 1993).

[7]The Book of Common Prayer.

Chapter 6: Practices for Opening to God Together

[1]Brian C. Taylor, *Spirituality for Everyday Living: An Adaptation of the Rule of St. Benedict* (Collegeville, Minn.: Liturgical Press, 1989), p. 12.

[2]The Transforming Community® experience is available to spiritual leaders through the Transforming Center. For more information, visit www.transformingcenter.org.

[3]Jim Loehr and Tony Schwartz, *The Power of Full Engagement* (New York: Free Press, 2003), pp. 4, 41, 5.

[4]For more complete liturgies for fixed-hour prayer visit the Transforming Center website at www.transformingcenter.org. You could also use *Hour by Hour,* a prayer book in the Anglican tradition; Phyllis Tickle's *The Divine Hours;* or *The Little Book of Hours: Praying with the Community of Jesus.*

[5]The Morning Prayer, Evening Prayer, and Opening and Benediction from

the Night Prayer are adapted from *The Upper Room Worshipbook,* ed. Elise Eslinger (Nashville: Upper Room Books, 1985, 2006). The Midday Prayer is adapted from the Book of Common Prayer.

Chapter 7: Practices for Listening to Each Other

[1]Robert Mulholland, from a personal note to the author, December 12, 2011.

[2]Brian Taylor, *Spirituality for Everyday Living* (Collegeville, Minn.: Liturgical Press, 1989), p. 17.

[3]Ibid., p. 19.

[4]Gareth Icenogle, *Biblical Foundations for Small Group Ministry* (Downers Grove, Ill.: InterVarsity Press, 1994), pp. 62, 63.

[5]The Iona Community, *Iona Abbey Worship Book* (Glasgow, U.K.: Wild Goose Publications, 2001), p. 183.

Chapter 8: A Covenant That Protects Community

[1]Gareth Icenogle, *Biblical Foundations for Small Group Ministry* (Downers Grove, Ill.: InterVarsity Press, 1994), p. 43.

[2]Charles Olsen and Ellen Morseth, *Selecting Church Leaders: A Practice in Spiritual Discernment* (Nashville: Upper Room Books, 2002), p. 21.

[3]The lines "so we lay down what is past and look to the future" are from The Iona Community, *Iona Abbey Worship Book* (Glasgow, U.K.: Wild Goose Publications, 2001).

[4]This prayer is adapted from the prayer we pray in the Transforming Center as we make our covenant together at the beginning of the Transforming Community experience.

Chapter 9: Get Ready

[1]For more on this key area for discernment see Charles Olsen and Ellen Morseth, *Selecting Church Leaders: A Practice in Spiritual Discernment* (Nashville: Upper Room Books, 2002).

[2]Paul Anderson, "The Meeting for Worship in Which Business is Conducted," *Quaker Religious Thought* 106-107 (November 2006): 29-30.

[3]Danny Morris and Charles Olsen, *Discerning God's Will Together* (Nashville: Upper Room Books, 1997), p. 60.

[4]Ibid., p. 61.

[5]Eden Grace, "An Introduction to Quaker Business Practice," delivered to the World Council of Churches, Ma'arat Saydnaya, Syria, March 2000.

[6]The Book of Common Prayer.

Chapter 10: Get Set

[1]John English, *Spiritual Intimacy and Community* (New York: Paulist Press, 1992), p. 111.

[2]Danny Morris and Charles Olsen, *Discerning God's Will Together: A Spiritual Practice for the Church* (Nashville: Upper Room Books, 1997), p. 76.

[3]Thomas R. Kelly, *A Testament of Devotion* (New York: HarperSanFrancisco, 1941), p. 31.

[4]The Book of Common Prayer.

Chapter 11: Go!

[1]Lon Fendall, Jan Wood and Bruce Bishop, *Practicing Discernment Together: Finding God's Way Forward in Decision Making* (Newberg, Ore.: Barclay Press, 2007), p. 96.

[2]Adapted from Suzanne Farnham, Stephanie Hull and Taylor McLean, *Grounded in God*, rev. ed. (Harrisburg, Penn.: Morehouse, 1999), p. 57.

[3]Charles Kingsley (1819-1875), quoted in Jeffery Rowthorne, comp., "Octave of Prayer in Preparation for General Convention 2006," 75th General Convention of the Protestant Episcopal Church in the U.S.A., June 2006.

[4]Fendall, Wood and Bishop, *Practicing Discernment Together*, p.134.

[5]Ernest Larkin, *Silent Presence* (Denville, N.J.: Dimension Books, 1981), p. 59.

[6]Unpublished comments from a Quaker pastor.

[7]The Book of Common Prayer.

Chapter 12: But Does It Work?

[1]Depending on the church polity and organizational structure, you may need to present what you have discerned to others in such a way that you invite them to discern the rightness of this as well.

[2]Jeffery Rowthorne, "Octave of Prayer in Preparation for General Convention 2006," 75th General Convention of the Protestant Episcopal Church in the U.S.A., June 2006, Day 5.

Appendix 1: Leader's Guide

[1]Pierre Teilhard de Chardin, quoted in Michael Harter, *Hearts on Fire: Praying with Jesuits* (St. Louis: Institute of Jesuit Sources, 1993), p. 58.

Appendix 2: A Biblical Perspective on Spiritual Transformation

[1]Richard Foster, *Renovaré Perspective*, April 1999.

[2]Robert Mulholland, *Invitation to a Journey* (Downers Grove, Ill.: InterVarsity Press, 1993), p. 145.

Appendix 3: *Lectio Divina*

[1]Dietrich Bonhoeffer, *Life Together* (New York: Harper SanFrancisco, 1954), pp. 81-82.

TRANSF◉RMING RESOURCES

A Ministry of the Transforming Center®

Resources to Help You Experience Spiritual Transformation

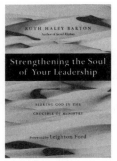

**Strengthening the Soul
of Your Leadership**
ISBN 978-0-8308-3513-3

Longing for More
ISBN 978-0-8308-3506-5

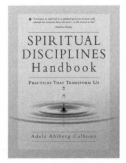

**Spiritual Disciplines
Handbook**
ISBN 978-0-8308-3330-6

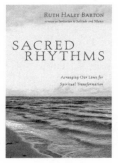

Sacred Rhythms
ISBN 978-0-8308-3333-7

Sacred Rhythms DVD
video download and
participant's guide
available from
www.Zondervan.com

**Invitation to Solitude
and Silence**
ISBN 978-0-8308-3545-4

**Invitation to Solitude
and Silence Audio Book**
available from
www.oasisaudio.com

Invitations from God
ISBN 978-0-8308-3553-9

www.transformingcenter.org

For more resources on **Pursuing God's Will Together,** *visit*
www.pursuinggodswilltogether.com

TRANSF🌀RMING CENTER®
Strengthening the Soul of Your Leadership

Learn more about spiritual transformation for pastors, Christian leaders and congregations

The Transforming Center exists to strengthen the souls of pastors, Christian leaders, and the congregations and organizations they serve. Don't just learn about spiritual transformation—experience it in your own life!

Ruth Haley Barton is the founder of the Transforming Center.

Visit the Transforming Center online to learn more about:

- Transforming Community®, our two-year experience of spiritual formation for leaders

- Earning a Doctor of Ministry, a master's specialization or a certificate in spiritual transformation

- Regional and national pastors' retreats

- Onsite teaching and spiritual guidance for your staff and elders

- Teaching and transformational experiences for your congregation

- Published resources—print and electronic

Join thousands of pastors and Christian leaders . . .

subscribe today to our free *eReflections*, spiritual guidance via email.

to subscribe, visit:

www.TransformingCenter.org

Transforming Center | 1600 Somerset Lane | Wheaton, IL 60189 | 630-588-8133

formatio

TRADITION. EXPERIENCE.
TRANSFORMATION.

Formatio books from InterVarsity Press follow the rich tradition of the church in the journey of spiritual formation. These books are not merely about being informed, but about being transformed by Christ and conformed to his image. Formatio stands in InterVarsity Press's evangelical publishing tradition by integrating God's Word with spiritual practice and by prompting readers to move from inward change to outward witness. InterVarsity Press uses the chambered nautilus for Formatio, a symbol of spiritual formation because of its continual spiral journey outward as it moves from its center. We believe that each of us is made with a deep desire to be in God's presence. Formatio books help us to fulfill our deepest desires and to become our true selves in light of God's grace.